South-Western

MEDIA MART

A Computer Activities Flow of Work Simulation

Karen Rhodes
Cypress Creek High School
Houston, Texas

Kim Sempe
Cypress Falls High School
Houston, Texas

John Steffee
Robert E. Lee High School
Tyler, Texas

Reviewer:

Patricia Herrera
Del Valle High School
El Paso, Texas

JOIN US ON THE INTERNET
WWW: http://www.thomson.com
EMAIL: findit@kiosk.thomson.com A service of I(T)P®

South-Western Educational Publishing
an International Thomson Publishing company I(T)P®

Cincinnati • Albany, NY • Belmont, CA • Bonn • Boston • Detroit • Johannesburg • London • Madrid
Melbourne • Mexico City • New York • Paris • Singapore • Tokyo • Toronto • Washington

Managing Editor: Janie F. Schwark
Project Manager: Dave Lafferty
Marketing Manager: John Wills
Production Services: Shepherd, Inc.
Production Editor: Lora Kalb

ISBN: 0-538-71816-1

2 3 4 5 6 7 8 9 H 00 99 98

Steffee, John.
Media mart: a computer activities flow of work simulation/John Steffee, Karen Rhodes, Kim Sempe.
p. cm.
ISBN 0-538-71813-7
1. Computer simulation. 2. Business—Computer simulation.
I. Rhodes, Karen, 1947- . II. Sempe, Kim. III. Title.
QA76.9.C65S75 1996
658.8'7' 0078553—dc21 96-37148
CIP

Printed in the United States of America

I(T)P
International Thomson Publishing

South-Western Educational Publishing is a division of International Thomson Publishing, Inc.
The ITP trademark is used under license.

Preface

OBJECTIVES

Media Mart is a generic computer simulation designed to fulfill a particular need—provide students with real-world activities in which they can apply previously learned computer skills. Unlike other information processing simulations, students work in *cooperative teams* of two to three students to manage and operate a retail business that sells entertainment equipment.

ORGANIZATION

Students make managerial-level decisions as they create and maintain the necessary records to operate their business. Each team competes with other teams in the class to earn the greatest net profit. There are thirty-six jobs in *Media Mart* simulating six months of business activity. *Media Mart* requires fifteen to thirty hours to complete, depending on the selection of optional activities.

The student template disk provides template files of document forms, spreadsheets, and other working papers.

An annotated teacher's manual and solutions disk accompanies the simulation. The manual includes instructional strategies, lesson plans, evaluation guidelines, tests, and solutions to jobs.

While designed primarily for business computer information systems classes, *Media Mart* can be used in similar computer classes. It is not necessary for each student to have his/her individual computer; several students can share a computer if necessary.

While completing the jobs in *Media Mart,* students will develop interpersonal skills as well as improve their problem-solving skills—skills that are highly sought-after in the business world!

ACKNOWLEDGMENTS

Many thanks to Cheryl Oswalt, Cypress Creek High School, Houston, Texas, and to Melissa Rouse, Lewisville High School, Lewisville, Texas, for their assistance in proofreading and editing.

A very special thank you to John Steffee for his original idea (*Mower Store*) and for sharing it with us. We discovered *Mower Store* several years ago, and it was love at first sight! We knew this was exactly the type of simulation we had in mind for our business computer applications classes. It has been a *huge* success; our students love it! We added many ideas and activities over the years until it evolved into *Media Mart*. We hope you have as much fun with it as we do!

Contents

**optional jobs

INTRODUCTION

You will be starting a small business that sells entertainment equipment. The business will operate for six months from July to December. Each business will be established as a partnership and will compete with other businesses to earn the greatest net profit. Net profit is the amount of money earned after all expenses are paid from sales. Your success will depend on good business decisions. Each business must keep accurate records and work as part of a cooperative team. Your group grade will be based on (1) following directions; (2) accuracy of records/documents; (3) completing your work on time.

Your business will sell the following six entertainment products.

	Stock Number
• **Portable CD Player**	PCD140
• **Deluxe Home Theater System**	DTS500
• **High-Power CD Deck**	HCD240
• **Surround Sound Speaker System**	SSS200
• **Mini-Stereo with Three Disc Changer**	MDC340
• **Six-Piece Home Theater System**	STS400

Several factors will affect and determine your sales. Product demand will change from month to month. Each business will purchase market research to forecast monthly sales for each product. You will select a vendor from which to buy inventory and then determine your markup and retail prices. Pricing is important because lower prices always attract customers. If your prices are too low, however, you will not earn enough profit to pay your business expenses. (It also costs money to run a business!)

Other factors that will influence sales and affect your net profit will be operating expenses such as rent, advertising, payroll, and store hours. Better locations cost more but attract more customers. The more you advertise, the more publicity your store gets. You must hire dependable employees and keep your store open long enough to create opportunity for shopping and sales. The more you spend on these items, the greater your expenses. The greater your expenses, the lower your net profit.

It will take good business decisions (and a little luck) to determine just the right amount to spend on these expenses to generate sales. ***Have fun and good luck!***

PRODUCT DESCRIPTION

		Stock Number
• **Portable CD Player**	—Car kit —Skip protection —Backlit display	PCD140
• **Deluxe Home Theater System**	—Receiver with 110 watts per channel in stereo with 4 audio and 2 video inputs —Center channel speaker —3-way front speaker —Rear speaker —10" powered subwoofer	DTS500
• **High-Power CD Deck**	—Detachable face —Wireless remote —30 watts x 4 channels —Control-capable CD changer	HCD240
• **Surround Sound Speaker System**	—Magnetically shielded center speaker —6 1/4 inch subwoofer —50 watts of power	SSS200
• **Mini-Stereo with Three-Disc Changer**	—3-disc carousel —Dual auto reverse cassette deck —AM/FM tuner —Remote —30 watts x 2	MDC340
• **Six-Piece Home Theater System**	—Receiver with 60 watts per channel in stereo —Center channel speaker —3-way front speaker —Rear speaker —8" powered subwoofer	STS400

TERMINOLOGY

COST OF GOODS SOLD—The amount a company paid for merchandise that was sold.

FICA TAX—Social Security tax.

GROSS PAY—Total salary before any deductions are subtracted (hours * rate).

GROSS PROFIT—The difference between sales revenue and cost of goods sold (before operating expenses are deducted).

INTEREST—The amount charged by the bank for the use of borrowed money.

LESSEE—A tenant under a lease of real property.

LESSOR—A landlord who leases real property to a tenant.

LIST PRICE—The price of goods in a supplier's catalog before any discounts are deducted.

MARKETING STRATEGY—A plan for selling a product.

MARKUP—The difference between the retail price and the cost price.

NET LOSS—The difference between sales revenue and expenses when expenses are greater than sales revenue.

NET PAY—The amount of money left after all deductions have been taken out of gross pay.

NET PROFIT—The difference between sales revenue and expenses when sales revenue is greater than expenses.

OPERATING EXPENSES—The usual maintenance expenses of a business (such as rent, salaries, advertising, etc.) other than the cost of buying merchandise for resale.

PRINCIPAL—The amount of money borrowed.

PURCHASES—Merchandise that a business buys from a wholesaler to resell at a retail price.

RETAIL PRICE—The final selling price paid for goods or services by the consumer.

REVENUE—Income earned from the sale of goods and/or services.

TRADE DISCOUNT—Two or more discounts deducted in succession from the list price.

VENDOR—A company, sometimes called a supplier, that supplies a retail business with products to be resold to the public.

WHOLESALE PRICE—The price a retailer pays to a vendor for merchandise (cost of goods sold).

WITHHOLDING TAX—The amount withheld from pay for federal income tax.

MAKEUP ASSIGNMENTS

For individual students to receive credit for the work done by their partners during one or more absence(s), he or she must complete a makeup assignment for *each day missed.* After more than seven excused or unexcused absences for *any* reason (field trips, college days, suspensions, etc.), you will be terminated from your company and must complete the remainder of the project *individually.*

ABSENCE:

#1. Create your own personal resume including your (1) education, (2) activities, (3) job skills, (4) work experience, and (5) references.

#2. Using your software's graphic features, design your own personal business card (to scale). Include your name, company name, complete address, telephone number, and one graphic and/or logo.

#3. Write a job description for your sales personnel. Describe the necessary qualifications and/or experience required, the type of work to be done, and where the job fits into the organizational and wage structure of your company.

#4. Use your software's graphic features to design a neighborhood value-pak coupon (to scale) for your company. Include important information such as your company name, address, phone number, type of products (see p. ix), and a minimum of one graphic.

#5. Using your word processing software, create a list of ten professional interview questions to use when interviewing applicants for sales positions.

#6. Create an employee evaluation form. Include appropriate dress, work habits (initiative, dependability, punctuality), selling skills, ability to get along with others, etc.

#7. Write a one-page report explaining how your company has done during the first three months of operation. What have been your net profits/losses? What changes (payroll, advertising, inventory) would you suggest for the next three months? Are partners working together cooperatively? What improvements are needed?

Job 1
Partnership Agreement

Instructions:

Open the **PARTNER** template and print. Using black or blue ink complete the Partnership Agreement form.

Make necessary decisions such as:

- Original name for your business
- Various responsibilities for each partner

PARTNERSHIP AGREEMENT

This Agreement made this ________________ day of ____________________,

Year____________________, between ____________________________________,

______________________________, ____________________________________,

and ____

all of the City of ______________________, County of ______________________,

State of ______________, witness and agree to the following:

1. ***Name:*** The company name of the partnership shall be ____.

2. ***Purpose:*** The purpose of the partnership shall be ____.

3. ***Duration:*** The partnership shall commence as of today and continue for a period of six months or until it is dissolved or liquidated.

4. ***Loans by Partners:*** Interest at the rate of ___________ percent per annum shall be allowed on all loans made to the partnership.

5. ***Time Devoted to Business:*** Each partner shall devote his/her entire time, attention, and ability to the affairs of the partnership.

6. ***Sickness:*** When a partner is unable to devote his/her full time to partnership affairs for reasons of health *or otherwise*, the remaining partners may by vote of the majority remove the said partner.

7. ***Management:*** Each partner shall have equal voice in the conduct of the affairs of the business and all decisions shall be by vote of the majority. ______________________ shall act as General Manager to administer the general affairs of the partnership and to carry out and put into effect the general policies and specific instructions of the majority of the partners.

8. ***Bank Accounts:*** The partnership shall maintain checking or other accounts in such bank as the partners shall agree upon. Withdrawal shall be on the signature of__________________ and co-signed by __________________.

Job 1 continues on page 2

9. ***Records:*** All books, records, and accounts of the partnership shall be maintained at the office of the partnership and shall be open to inspection at all times by all partners. At the end of each month, the books shall be balanced and financial statements shall be prepared and made available to each partner posting the results of operations during the previous month.

10. ***Salaries:*** Until further agreed upon, no partner shall draw a salary until the original bank loan is repaid and the business has sufficient working capital.

11. ***Profits and Losses:*** The partners shall share equally in the profits and losses. As soon as practical after the accounting statements for the fiscal year are approved by all partners, the profits shall be paid to the partners, provided there are funds available in excess of the working capital requirements.

12. ***Limitations on Partners:*** No partner, without the consent of all other partners, shall borrow money on the partnership name for partnership purposes or utilize collateral owned by the partnership as security for such loans; assign, transfer, pledge, compromise, or release any of the claims or debts due to the partnership except on payment in full; consent to the arbitration of any dispute or controversy of the partnership; transfer company assets; make, execute, or deliver any assignment for the benefits of creditors; make, execute, or deliver any contract to sell, bill of sale, deed, mortgage, or lease relating to any substantial part of the partnership assets or his interest therein; or engage in any business or occupation without the consent of all other partners.

IN WITNESS WHEREOF, the parties have signed and sealed this Agreement

this ____________________ day of ________________, Year_______________.

Signatures:

______________________________ ______________________________

______________________________ ______________________________

Job 2
Letterhead

Instructions:

Using your word processing software, create an original letterhead for your company within the upper 2 inches of the page. Change the top and bottom margins to .5 inch and include font/size changes, a graphic image, etc. Use your own original company name and make up an address. Save as **J2LTHD** and print.

COMPANY NAME
Street Address
City. State ZIP
Telephone No.

Job 3
Business Plan

Instructions:

Using your word processing software, open **J2LTHD** and save as **J3BSPLAN.** Using the guidelines shown, make the necessary decisions to create your own business plan.

- Select at least two marketing strategies
- Decide on the types of advertising and how much to spend
- Decide how many employees to hire
- Decide on store hours/days

Resave and print.

Terms:
Marketing Strategy

BUSINESS PLAN

I. MARKETING STRATEGIES

A. In-store displays
B. Discount coupons
C. Special sales
D. Telemarketing

II. ADVERTISING (Monthly budget range $500 - $2500)

A. Radio (10-second clips $250 per day--average 10 clips)
B. Television (30-second spots)
Day: 5 a.m.-6 p.m.: $1500--3 spots
Prime: 7 p.m.-9 p.m.: $2500--1 spot
Late: 9 p.m.-5 a.m.: $2000--3 spots
C. Newspaper (2x3 inch ad is $300 a day in a metropolitan paper)
(2x3 inch ad is $75 a day in a suburban/local paper)
D. Direct Mail (28 cents per colored printed mailed page)
E. Billboards & Signs (Rent-A-Sign portable--$150 per week)
(Billboard--large $500 per week; small $500 per month)
F. Special Promotions: Grand Opening prizes, soft drinks, etc.

III. NUMBER OF PART-TIME EMPLOYEES (2-4)

Note: By hiring part-time employees for the first six months, who work less than 40 hours a week, you will avoid paying benefits such as medical insurance, etc.

IV. STORE HOURS/DAYS OF WEEK

Job 4
Bank Letter

Instructions:

Using your word processing software, open **J2LTHD** and save as **J4BNKLTR.** Write a letter to a banker applying for financing to start your business. Resave and print.

BANK LETTER

After consulting with experienced business leaders at your local Chamber of Commerce, you have determined that $50,000 will be required to start your business. You will have to borrow the start-up capital.

Using your word processing software and previously created letterhead, write a letter to a local bank applying for a small business loan of $50,000. Be sure to emphasize the opportunities for this type of business in your community. Your letter should also include your (1) marketing strategies; (2) advertising plans; (3) number of part-time employees; and (4) store hours. Refer to your Business Plan and the example below:

Current date

First Bank, Inc.
1000 State Street
Your City, State ZIP

Ladies and Gentlemen:

¶1: State the nature of the request--to apply for a small business loan of $50,000.

¶2: Provide explanatory details (see steps 1-4 above).

¶3: Provide a goodwill closing.

Sincerely yours,

Xxxxxx Xxxxxx
General Manager

Job 5
Loan Spreadsheet Template

Instructions:

Using your spreadsheet software, open the LOAN template and enter formulas to calculate the cost of three loan options. Circle your company's choice. Save as **J5LOAN** and print.

Terms:
Principal
Interest

CALCULATING THE COST OF A LOAN

Your small business loan will be for a period of six months with an interest rate of 11%. The principal is ($50,000) the amount borrowed; interest is the amount charged for using the bank's money. Open the **LOAN.XLS** template and use the payment function of your spreadsheet software to calculate the total cost of the loan for each of three payment options. The bank, however, will make the final decision.

OPTION 1: Six monthly payments of principal and interest

Principal	Interest Rate	Number of Payments	Monthly Payment	Total Payments	Cost of Loan
$50,000	11%	6			

OPTION 2: One payment of principal and interest due at the end of six months

Principal	Interest Rate	Number of Payments	Total Interest	Total Payment	Cost of Loan
$50,000	11%	1			

OPTION 3: Six monthly interest payments with principal due at the end of six months

Principal	Interest Rate	Number of Payments	One Month's Interest	Total Payments	Cost of Loan
$50,000	11%	6			

Job 6
Location Spreadsheet Template

Instructions:

Using your spreadsheet software, open the **LOCATION** template and enter formulas to determine the monthly cost of the location choices. Circle your company's choice. Save as **J6LOCAT** and print.

LOCATION TEMPLATE

K & K Realty Company has several strip centers in the city with vacancies. They have decided to offer a special rate for first-time business owners. Major retailers are already located and established in each of the strip centers.

® **Area A** is located on the front corner of the strip center in a high-traffic area facing a main highway and has two window displays.
® **Area B** is located on the left corner and has two windows, one facing a side street.
® **Area C** is located on the inside of the strip center with one window display facing the parking lot.

ALL LOCATIONS ARE 20 BY 25 FEET.

You will sign a lease and remain in that location for six months.

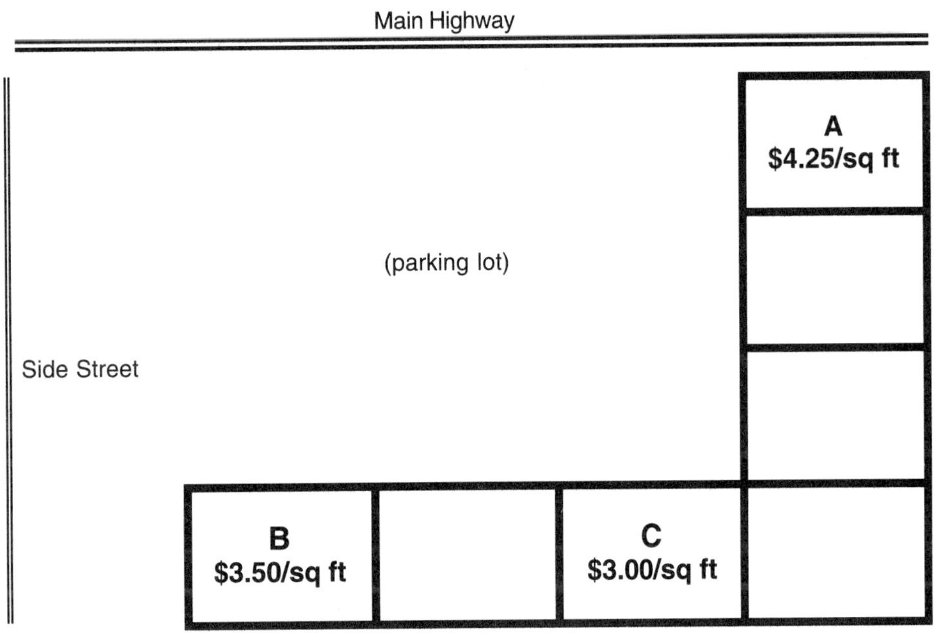

Job 7

Lease Agreement Form

Instructions:

Open the **LEASE** template and print. Using black or blue ink, complete the Lease Agreement form.

Terms:

Lessor

Lessee

K & K REALTY COMPANY
Agreement of Lease

The State of ______________________ County of ______________________

Made this ______________ day of ______________ A.D. Year _____ by and between

____, known as LESSOR

and ____, known as LESSEE

Witnesseth, That the said Lessor does by these presents Lease and Demise unto the said Lessee the following described property to-wit Lying and being situated in the County of ____________

State of ____________________ for the term of ____________________ beginning

the ____________________ day of ________________ year ________ and ending

the ____________________ day of ________________ year ________ paying the

sum of ____ dollars.

Upon the conditions and covenants following:

First: *The Lessee will punctually pay said rents and deliver up said premises on the day of the expiration of this lease, in as good condition as the same were in when received.*

Second: *The Lessee shall take good care of the property and its fixtures and no improvements or alterations shall be made in or to the hereby demised premises without the consent of the Lessor in writing.*

Third: *The Lessee shall promptly execute and fulfill all the ordinances of the city corporation applicable to said premises and all orders and requirements imposed by any governing bodies at the Lessee's expense.*

Fourth: *The Lessee shall not sub-let said premises, or any part thereof, to any person or persons whatsoever, without the consent of said Lessor, in writing.*

Fifth: *The Lessor shall not be liable to Lessee or to Lessee's employees, patrons, or visitors, for any damage to person or property, caused by the act of negligence of any other tenant of said demised premises, or due to the building on said premises.*

Sixth: *The Lessee shall not place any signs at, on, or about the premises except as and where first approved by the Lessor; and the Lessor shall have the right to remove any sign or signs in order to paint the building or premises or make any other repairs or alterations.*

Seventh: *On failure to pay the rent in advance, or comply with any of the foregoing obligations, or in violation of any of the foregoing covenants, the Lessor may declare the lease forfeited at Lessor's discretion and Lessor or Lessor's agent or attorney shall have the power to enter and hold, occupy and repossess the entire premises herein before described, as before the execution of these presents.*

IN TESTIMONY WHEREOF, The parties to this agreement have hereunto set their hands in duplicate, the day and year above written.

______________________________ ______________________________
LESSOR LESSEE

Job 8
Work Schedule Forms

Instructions:

Task 1: Manager Work Schedule

Open the **M3SCHED** template and print. Using pen or pencil, list partners' names in alphabetical order on the indicated blanks to determine job rotation for each manager. Staple this form to the inside cover of your folder for future reference and use. (If there are only two students in the group, open the template **M2SCHED.**)

MANAGER WORK SCHEDULE

Manager #1 ________________________________

Manager #2 ________________________________

Manager #3 ________________________________

JOB	*JULY*	*AUG*	*SEPT*	*OCT*	*NOV*	*DEC*
Payroll	1	2	3	1	2	3
Inventory	2	3	1	2	3	1
Cash Flow	3	1	2	3	1	2
Monthly Audit	1	2	3	1	2	3
Data Input	2	3	1	2	3	1
Income Statement	3	1	2	3	1	2

When you finish your job, initial the box below:

COMPLETED MONTHLY JOBS						
JOB	*JULY*	*AUG*	*SEPT*	*OCT*	*NOV*	*DEC*
Update Payroll						
Update Inventory						
Update Cash Flow						
Update Monthly Audit						
Complete Data Input						
Complete Inventory						
Complete Cash Flow						
Complete Income						
Complete Monthly Audit						

Job 8 continues on page 10

Task 2: Employee Work Schedule

Open the **EMPLSCHD** template and print. Using pencil, complete the form to determine the number of hours each part-time employee will work.

EMPLOYEE WORK SCHEDULE

COMPANY NAME ____________________ **MONTH** ________

Store Hours

____

Employee #1 ________	Weekly Hours Worked _____	Employee #3 ________	Weekly Hours Worked _____
Employee #2 ________	Hours Worked _____	Employee #4 ________	Hours Worked _____

	SUN	MON	TUES	WED	THURS	FRI	SAT
7:00 AM							
7:30							
8:00							
8:30							
9:00							
9:30							
10:00							
10:30							
11:00							
11:30							
12:00 PM							
12:30							
1:00							
1:30							
2:00							
2:30							
3:00							
3:30							
4:00							
4:30							
5:00							
5:30							
6:00							
6:30							
7:00							
7:30							
8:00							
8:30							
9:00							

Note: 8 hours scheduled includes a 30-minute lunch break.
Less than 8 hours does not include a lunch break.
All other breaks are on company time.

Job 9

Payroll Spreadsheet Template—July

Instructions:

Using your spreadsheet software, open the **PAYROLL** template and enter data/formulas to complete the July payroll for your company. Save as **MPAYROLL** and print.

Terms:

Gross Pay

Withholding Tax

FICA Tax

Net Pay

MONTHLY PAYROLL

Each month you will use your spreadsheet software to calculate your monthly payroll. Refer to the Employee Work Schedule to enter the hours of your part-time employees. If sales are projected to go up for the month, then you should increase employee hours or vice versa. Remember that as a new business you cannot afford to pay benefits such as medical insurance. Therefore, when scheduling hours, do **not** allow any employee to work more than 39 hours per week or 8 hours a day.

You must pay the minimum wage of $5.15 per hour, but as a new business you cannot afford to pay more than $6.25 per hour. To avoid employee morale problems, it is a good policy to start all new employees at the same base rate. You may give a raise after a certain period of time (i.e., three months of satisfactory job performance).

Open the **PAYROLL** template and enter the hours and pay rate for each employee. Then enter formulas to calculate the following:

1. Total the weekly hours for each employee
2. GROSS PAY = Total Hours * Pay Rate
3. WITHHOLDING TAX (15%) = Gross Pay * 15%
4. FICA TAX (7.65%) = Gross Pay * 7.65%
5. NET PAY = Gross Pay - (WH Tax + FICA Tax)
6. Add the columns to get weekly totals
7. MONTHLY TOTAL HOURS = Weekly Total * 4
8. MONTHLY NET PAY = Weekly Total * 4

				COMPANY NAME									
				PAYROLL FOR MONTH OF ?									
								TOTAL	PAY	GROSS	WH	FICA	NET
EMPLOYEE	SUN	MON	TUE	WED	THUR	FRI	SAT	HOURS	RATE	PAY	TAX	TAX	PAY
Employee #1													
Employee #2								<40	($5.15-$6.25)				
Employee #3													
Employee #4													
WEEKLY TOTALS								####		####	####	####	####
MONTHLY TOTALS								####					####

Job 10
Employee Work Rules

Instructions:

Using your word processing software, open **J2LTHD** and save as **J10ERULS.** Create a minimum of eight rules for your company following the guidelines. Use complete sentences. Resave and print.

EMPLOYEE WORK RULES

Every business should have specific employee work rules so that employees know exactly what is expected. Use the guidelines below to create appropriate rules for your employees. Additional topics may be added.

COMPANY NAME
EMPLOYEE WORK RULES

1. Appropriate dress
2. Personal telephone calls
3. Absences and sick days
4. Number and length of breaks, including lunch
5. Raises--How much? How often?
6. On-the-job training:
   A. Knowledge of equipment
   B. Using the cash register
   C. Dealing with customers
7. Safety guidelines
8. Procedures for dealing with infractions of the above rules

Job 11
Market Research Contract Form

Instructions:

Open the **RESEARCH** template and print. Using black or blue ink, complete the contract.

R-S-S MARKET RESEARCH, INC.
SERVICE AGREEMENT

How much should you order?

What will be the big seller this month?

The correct answers to these questions could mean the difference between the success and failure of your business. How much money do you earn from customers who want to buy your product if it is out of stock? Not one dime! How much money does your inventory cost if it does not sell? Plenty! (Unless, of course, you have a banker that loans you money for free).

Having the right merchandise at the right time means your cash register rings. Ordering merchandise that doesn't sell means the cash register rings -- for your supplier and your banker.

What it boils down to is this: **Whose cash register do you want to ring?**

R-S-S MARKET RESEARCH, INC. will provide the information you need. Each month you will receive information of what's hot and what's not. Based on our thorough market research, you will know BEFORE YOU ORDER what products are likely to sell each month and the number of each product you are likely to sell.

What is the price of this fantastic service? Only $200 per month. For only $200 a month, you can see the future and predict - SUCCESS!

- -

Yes, we want this invaluable service.

Our company, ______________________________, agrees to pay the sum of $200 per month to R-S-S MARKET RESEARCH, INC. for data predicting the products that will sell best each month.

______________________________	______________________________
NAME	DATE

R-S-S MARKET RESEARCH, INC. assumes no responsibility for accuracy of data.

Job 12

Sales Forecast Spreadsheet Template

Instructions:

Using your spreadsheet software, open the **FORECAST** template and enter formulas to complete the estimated monthly sales. Save as **J12FCAST** and print.

- POP RATIO = 100000/Population
- 2 decimal places
- Copy down for each month
- PROJ = $B4 * D4
- Copy and paste across for each product
- Copy and paste down for each month

SALES FORECAST

Using your spreadsheet software, open the **FORECAST** template. This data, provided by R-S-S Market Research, Inc. shows past sales of your six products in cities with populations ranging from 35,000 to 255,000. Your business is located in a community with a population of approximately 100,000. Therefore, to use these past sales figures, you must first enter a formula in B4 to calculate the population ratio (HINT: 100000/Population). To calculate projected sales for each product, multiply the population ratio times the previous sales figure. This formula can be entered once in **E4** and copied to all other locations if the ***POP RATIO* column reference** is entered as an **absolute (i.e. $B4*D4)**. You will use this information to determine how many units of each product to order every month.

	A	B	C	D	E	F	G	H	I	J	K	L	M	N	O
1		*POP*		*PCD140*	*PCD140*	*DTS500*	*DTS500*	*HCD240*	*HCD240*	*SSS200*	*SSS200*	*MDC340*	*MDC340*	*STS400*	*STS400*
2	*POPULATION*	*RATIO*	*MONTH*	*SALES*	*PROJ*	*SALES*	*PROJ*	*SALES*	*PROJ*	*SALES*	*PROJ*	*SALES*	*PROJ*	*SALES*	*PROJ*
3															
4	35000		July	0		1		2		2		1		2	
5	72000		July	0		1		6		3		4		0	
6	135000		July	7		4		11		8		5		4	
7	149000		July	6		4		6		6		6		5	
8	180000		July	8		5		7		8		11		7	
9	255000		July	10		13		15		15		12		20	
10															
11	35000		Aug	1		2		2		2		1		3	
12	72000		Aug	1		4		7		4		7		0	
13	135000		Aug	10		5		15		10		8		4	
14	149000		Aug	9		7		9		9		10		6	
15	180000		Aug	11		8		11		12		20		7	
16	255000		Aug	15		12		12		22		20		5	
17															
18	35000		Sept	2		2		2		3		3		2	
19	72000		Sept	2		4		7		6		12		0	
20	135000		Sept	17		8		13		13		10		4	
21	149000		Sept	15		9		7		12		15		5	
22	180000		Sept	19		10		10		16		20		7	
23	255000		Sept	25		17		12		30		33		15	
24															
25	35000		Oct	2		3		2		4		4		2	
26	72000		Oct	3		7		8		7		14		0	
27	135000		Oct	20		10		15		13		11		4	
28	149000		Oct	16		12		10		15		15		6	
29	180000		Oct	21		17		14		21		20		8	
30	255000		Oct	30		25		15		37		50		26	
31															
32	35000		Nov	3		3		3		4		5		5	
33	72000		Nov	3		6		12		8		15		0	
34	135000		Nov	26		11		20		13		9		10	
35	149000		Nov	22		12		12		18		15		13	
36	180000		Nov	29		17		14		25		20		17	
37	255000		Nov	40		25		23		45		50		38	
38															
39	35000		Dec	4		4		5		6		5		5	
40	72000		Dec	5		10		21		13		15		0	
41	135000		Dec	31		16		20		13		11		17	
42	149000		Dec	22		18		22		22		15		23	
43	180000		Dec	30		17		14		25		20		24	
44	255000		Dec	50		35		35		50		50		48	
45															

Job 13
Vendor Spreadsheet Template

Instructions:

Using your spreadsheet software, open the **VENDOR** template and enter formulas to determine from which vendor to buy products for the next six months. Circle your company's choice. (This is a six-month contract and will not change from month to month.) Save as **J13VNDR** and print.

Terms:
List Price
Chain Discount

SELECTING A VENDOR

A vendor is a company which supplies a retail business with products to be re-sold to the public. Your company will choose one of the three vendors listed below. **Once a vendor (supplier) is selected, all of your purchases for the next six months must be made from this vendor at the selected price.**

VENDOR #1: ***Ashton Suppliers*** sells their products at the **list price.** The price listed is your actual cost for the product.

VENDOR #2: ***Lakeland Wholesale*** uses a series of **trade discounts**, which is a special deduction from the list price. The use of a trade discount serves as a simple method of adjusting prices. When prices are rising, the manufacturer can drop one or more discounts from a series. Likewise, when prices are falling, a manufacturer can adjust prices by increasing the rate of the discount. Lakeland gives its customers a series of **three** trade discounts--10%, 6%, 3%.

EXAMPLE:

List Price	$320.00
Less 10%	-32.00
Result	**288.00**
Less 6%	-17.28
Result	**270.72**
Less 3%	-8.12
Net Cost	**262.60**

VENDOR #3: ***Sanchez Wholesale*** prices are based on the **quantity** purchased. The greater the quantity purchased, the lower the price. However, Sanchez Wholesale prices are based on your first order. **You will lock in the price for a product which will remain the same for the next six months regardless of the quantity ordered.**

COMPANY NAME
VENDOR PRICES

ASHTON		LAKELAND				SANCHEZ WHOLESALE			
			LESS 10%	LESS 6%	LESS 3%	COST FOR QUANTITY ORDERED			
PRODUCT	LIST PRICE	LIST PRICE				1-5	6-10	11-15	16-20
PCD140	$ 70.00	$ 79.20				$ 75.00	$ 72.00	$ 69.00	$ 67.00
DTS500	$ 700.00	$ 850.00				$ 710.00	$ 690.00	$ 680.00	$ 670.00
HCD240	$ 250.00	$ 300.00				$ 260.00	$ 249.00	$ 245.00	$ 240.00
SSS200	$ 120.00	$ 149.00				$ 130.00	$ 125.00	$ 120.00	$ 115.00
MDC340	$ 220.00	$ 259.00				$ 230.00	$ 220.00	$ 210.00	$ 200.00
STS400	$ 450.00	$ 549.00				$ 460.00	$ 455.00	$ 450.00	$ 445.00

Job 14

Store Policy

Instructions:

Using your word processing software, open **J2LTHD** and save as **J14SPLCY.** Create an appropriate store policy for your company using the guidelines shown. Use complete sentences and at least an 18 pt. font. Resave and print.

STORE POLICY

So that customers know what to expect when they make a purchase, many retail businesses display their store policy near the check-out or customer service area. Develop your store policy sign using the guidelines below:

COMPANY NAME

STORE POLICY

1. Type of identification required for checks? Picture ID? Manager approval required for checks over a certain amount?
2. Fee charged for returned checks? How much?
3. Which ***major*** credit cards are accepted?
4. Return policy:
   - receipt required?
   - length of time returns will be accepted?
   - condition of returned merchandise?
   - full refund or store credit?

Job 15

Inventory Spreadsheet Template—July

Instructions:

Using your spreadsheet software, open the **INVEN** template and enter data/formulas to complete July Inventory for your company. Save as **INVENTRY** and print.

Terms:

Cost
Markup
Retail Price
Purchases

INVENTORY

Keeping accurate inventory records is very important. Maintaining the correct inventory balance can mean the difference between the success or failure of your business. You always must be aware of what is in stock and what you need to order. You can sell only what you have in stock; low inventory means lost sales. Too much inventory sitting on the shelf and not selling will cost you money because you are paying interest on the money you borrowed.

Each month you will decide how much to mark up the cost of each product. To earn a profit, the minimum markup should be at least 60% of the cost; the maximum markup will be 100%. The markup does not have to be the same for each product, and you may change it from month to month. Remember to refer to your Sales Forecast each month to see which products will be the top sellers.

Open the **INVEN** template and (1) enter your cost and (2) the amount of the markup for each of the products. Next, enter formulas to make the following calculations:

1. RETAIL PRICE = (Our Cost * Markup) + Our Cost
2. BEGINNING INVENTORY - For the first month, the beginning inventory will be zero (0) for each item. For each succeeding month, the beginning inventory should be the same as the *ending inventory of the previous month.*
3. NUMBER ORDERED - Refer to your Sales Forecast (Job 12) and enter the number ordered for each item.
4. NUMBER SOLD - Enter zeros until you receive the monthly sales results. At the end of each month, you will enter the number sold for each item.
5. ENDING INVENTORY = Beginning Inventory + Number Ordered - Number Sold
6. PURCHASES = Our Cost * Number Ordered
7. SALES = Retail Price * Number Sold
8. COST OF GOODS SOLD = Our Cost * Number Sold
9. GROSS PROFIT = Sales - Cost of Goods Sold
10. TOTALS - Enter formulas to total the Purchases, Sales, Cost of Goods Sold, and Gross Profit columns.

Job 15 continues on page 18

			COMPANY NAME				
			INVENTORY FOR MONTH OF ?				
	OUR	MARKUP	RETAIL	BEGIN	NUM	NUM	END
ITEM	COST	%	PRICE	INV	ORDER	SOLD	INV
PCD140				0			
DTS500				0			
HCD240				0			
SSS200				0			
MDC340				0			
STS400				0			
					COST OF		
					GOODS		GROSS
ITEM	PURCHASES		SALES		SOLD		PROFIT
PCD140							
DTS500							
HCD240							
SSS200							
MDC340							
STS400							
TOTALS	####		####		####		####

Job 16

Cash Flow Spreadsheet Template—July

Instructions:

Using your spreadsheet software, open the **CASH** template and enter data/formulas to complete the July Cash Flow for your company. Save as **CASHFLOW** and print.

Terms:
Operating Expenses

CASH FLOW

The purpose of the cash flow statement is to maintain an exact record of cash. You should always know how much cash you have available to purchase inventory and to pay monthly operating expenses. When you purchase inventory, allow enough remaining cash to cover monthly operating expenses.

Open the **CASH** template and follow the instructions below:

1. Enter the cash balance from the previous month. For the first month (July), this amount will be $50,000, the amount borrowed to begin the business.

2. Enter the amount spent to purchase inventory (from INVENTRY).

3. Enter and total the amounts of the various operating expenses.

    a. Advertising Expense will be between $500-$2,500 and can be changed each month.

    b. Payroll Expense will be the **monthly net pay total** (from MPAYROLL).

    c. Rent Expense will be the same each month:
    Loc A = $2,125; Loc B = $1,750; Loc C = $1,500 (from J6LOCAT)

    d. The following expenses will be the same each month:

Market Research Expense	$200.00
Interest Expense	$458.33
Miscellaneous Expense	$500.00

4. To calculate Cash Before Sales, enter a formula to subtract Purchases and Total Expenses from Cash From Previous Month.

5. For Total Sales enter the Inventory Sales Total amount (from INVENTRY).

6. To find the Cash Balance, add Cash Before Sales and Total Sales. (For the next month, this Cash Balance will be carried forward and entered as the *Cash From Previous Month.*)

	COMPANY NAME			
	CASH FLOW FOR MONTH OF ?			
Cash From Previous Month			$ 50,000.00	
Purchases		####		
OPERATING EXPENSES:				
Advertising Expense				
Payroll Expense				
Rent Expense				
Market Research Expense	$ 200.00			
Interest Expense	$ 458.33			
Misc. Expense	$ 500.00			
Total Expenses		####		
Cash Before Sales			####	
Total Sales			INVENTRY SALES TOTAL	
Cash Balance			####	

Job 17

Monthly Audit Form—July

Instructions:

Open the **AUDTFORM** template and print. Using pencil, complete the preliminary part of the Monthly Audit Form for July.

MONTHLY AUDIT

The Monthly Audit Form will be used as as auditing device to check all figures. This form will combine data from the three main spreadsheets: Inventory, Cash, and Income.

You will only be able to complete part of the Monthly Audit form before the sales results. Complete the following sections, the remainder of the form will be left blank.

INVENTORY: Cost, Retail, Beginning Inventory, Number Order, Total Inventory
CASH: Cash from previous month, purchases, total expenses, Cash before sales

After the sales results are received, finish completing the Monthly Audit form.

MONTHLY AUDIT FORM

MONTH: ______________

COMPANY NAME:

____

INVENTORY

Product	Cost	Retail	Beginning Inventory	Number Order	Total Inventory	Number Sold	Ending Inventory
1. PCD140							
2. DTS500							
3. HCD240							
4. SSS200							
5. MDC340							
6. STS400							

CASH FLOW

Cash from Previous Month	______________	
Purchases (minus)	______________	-
Total Expenses (minus)	______________	-
Cash Before Sales (equals)	______________	=
Total Sales (plus)	______________	+
Cash Balance (equals)	______________	=

INCOME STATEMENT

Total Sales	______________	
Cost of Goods Sold (minus)	______________	-
Gross Profit (equals)	______________	=
Total Expenses (minus)	______________	-
Net Profit (equals)	______________	=

Job 18
Data Input Form—July

Instructions:

Open the **INPTFORM** template and print the 2-page form for all 6 months. Using blue or black ink, complete the Data Input Form for July.

DATA INPUT

The Data Input Form will be used by your teacher to generate the sales results. To complete this form use the Inventory, Cash, and Payroll spreadsheets.

Company Name: ______________________

DATA INPUT FORM

MONTH: July

Location $__________ Advertising $__________

Monthly Payroll $__________ Monthly Payroll Hours __________

Product	Retail Price	Total Inventory
1. PCD140	________	________
2. DTS500	________	________
3. HCD240	________	________
4. SSS200	________	________
5. MDC340	________	________
6. STS400	________	________

MONTH: August

Location $__________ Advertising $__________

Monthly Payroll $__________ Monthly Payroll Hours __________

Product	Retail Price	Total Inventory
1. PCD140	________	________
2. DTS500	________	________
3. HCD240	________	________
4. SSS200	________	________
5. MDC340	________	________
6. STS400	________	________

MONTH: September

Location $__________ Advertising Dollars $__________

Monthly Payroll $__________ Monthly Payroll Hours __________

Product	Retail Price	Total Inventory
1. PCD140	________	________
2. DTS500	________	________
3. HCD240	________	________
4. SSS200	________	________
5. MDC340	________	________
6. STS400	________	________

Job 19
Newspaper Advertisement or Flyer

Instructions:

Using your word processing software, create an original one-page newspaper advertisement or a one-page flyer for your company using the guidelines shown. Save as **J19AD** and print.

NEWSPAPER ADVERTISEMENT
or
FLYER

Using your word processing software, create **one** of the following:
- ♦ One full-page advertisement to appear in the local newspaper
- ♦ One full-page flyer to be placed on cars in the parking lot

Include the following information:

1. Complete company name, address, and phone number.
2. Store hours
3. Names of products:
   - ♦ Portable CD Player
   - ♦ Deluxe Home Theater System
   - ♦ High-Power CD Deck
   - ♦ Surround Sound Speaker System
   - ♦ Mini-Stereo with Three Disc Changer
   - ♦ Six-Piece Home Theater System
4. At least 3 font/size changes
5. Borders
6. At least 1 graphic image

Job 20
Finish July

Instructions:

Task 1: Update Inventory Spreadsheet

Using your spreadsheet software, open **INVENTRY**—July and enter number sold from the results printout. Save and print.

			COMPANY NAME				
			INVENTORY FOR MONTH OF ?				
	OUR	MARKUP	RETAIL	BEGIN	NUM	NUM	END
ITEM	COST	%	PRICE	INV	ORDER	SOLD	INV
PCD140				0			
DTS500				0			
HCD240				0			
SSS200				0			
MDC340				0			
STS400				0			
					COST OF		
					GOODS		GROSS
ITEM	PURCHASES		SALES		SOLD		PROFIT
PCD140							
DTS500							
HCD240							
SSS200							
MDC340							
STS400							
TOTALS	####		####		####		####

Task 2: Update Cash Flow Spreadsheet

Using your spreadsheet software, open **CASHFLOW**—July and enter SALES TOTAL from the inventory spreadsheet. Save and print.

	COMPANY NAME			
	CASH FLOW FOR MONTH OF ?			
Cash From Previous Month			$ 50,000.00	
Purchases		####		
OPERATING EXPENSES:				
Advertising Expense				
Payroll Expense				
Rent Expense				
Market Research Expense	$ 200.00			
Interest Expense	$ 458.33			
Misc. Expense	$ 500.00			
Total Expenses		####		
Cash Before Sales			####	
Total Sales			INVENTRY SALES TOTAL	
Cash Balance			####	

Job 20 continues on page 24

Task 3: Finalize Monthly Audit Form

Using pencil, complete the Monthly Audit Form and compare those figures with the completed Cash Flow and Inventory Statement.

MONTHLY AUDIT FORM

MONTH: ____________

COMPANY NAME:

____

INVENTORY

Product	Cost	Retail	Beginning Inventory	Number Order	Total Inventory	Number Sold	Ending Inventory
1. PCD140							
2. DTS500							
3. HCD240							
4. SSS200							
5. MDC340							
6. STS400							

CASH FLOW

Cash from Previous Month	____________	
Purchases (minus)	____________	-
Total Expenses (minus)	____________	-
Cash Before Sales (equals)	____________	=
Total Sales (plus)	____________	+
Cash Balance (equals)	____________	=

INCOME STATEMENT

Total Sales	____________	
Cost of Goods Sold (minus)	____________	-
Gross Profit (equals)	____________	=
Total Expenses (minus)	____________	-
Net Profit (equals)	____________	=

Task 4: Income Spreadsheet Template

Using your spreadsheet software, open the **INCOME** template and enter data/formulas to complete the July Income Statement for your company. Information should be obtained from the inventory and cash flow spreadsheets. Save as **INCOMEST** and print.

Terms:

Cost of Goods Sold
Overhead
Operating Expenses
Gross Profit
Net Profit
Revenue

INCOME STATEMENT

The income statement reports net profit or net loss over a certain period of time. The income statement also lists all the business's revenue and expenses. When total revenue is greater than total expenses, the business has earned a net profit. Conversely, if total expenses are greater than total revenue, the business has incurred a net loss.

Open the **INCOME** template and follow the instructions below:

1. Using your Inventory **individual** Sales figures, enter the amount of revenue earned from the sale of each product.
2. To calculate Total Sales, enter a formula to add the Revenue column.
3. Referring to your Inventory, enter the Cost of Goods Sold **Total** as indicated.
4. Enter a formula to calculate Gross Profit: (Total Sales - Cost of Goods Sold).
5. Referring to your Cash Flow Statement, enter the Operating Expenses as indicated.
6. To calculate Total Expenses, enter a formula to add the Operating Expenses column.
7. Enter a formula to calculate Net Profit/Loss: (Gross Profit - Total Expenses).

Job 20 continues on page 26

	COMPANY NAME		
INCOME STATEMENT FOR MONTH OF ?			
REVENUE:			
PCD140	INVENTRY SALES		
DTS500			
HCD240			
SSS200			
MDC340			
STS400			
TOTAL SALES		#####	
Cost of Goods Sold		INVENTRY TOTAL	
Gross Profit			#####
OPERATING EXPENSES:			
Advertising Expense	CASHFLOW		
Payroll Expense			
Rent Expense			
Market Research Exp.	$200.00		
Interest Expense	$458.33		
Misc. Expense	$500.00		
Total Expenses			#####
Net Profit/Loss			#####

Job 21

Begin August

Instructions:

Task 1: Payroll Spreadsheet

Open **MPAYROLL** and copy the spreadsheet from July tab to August tab. Make decisions and changes for August such as:

- Change Hours Worked
- Hire or fire employee?

Save and print.

				COMPANY NAME									
				PAYROLL FOR MONTH OF ?									
								TOTAL	PAY	GROSS	WH	FICA	NET
EMPLOYEE	SUN	MON	TUE	WED	THUR	FRI	SAT	HOURS	RATE	PAY	TAX	TAX	PAY
Employee #1													
Employee #2								<40	($5.15-$6.25)				
Employee #3													
Employee #4													
WEEKLY TOTALS								####		####	####	####	####
MONTHLY TOTALS								####					####

Task 2: Inventory Spreadsheet

Open **INVENTRY** and copy the spreadsheet from July tab to August tab.

- Transfer Ending Inventory for July to Beginning Inventory for August
- Enter "zeros" in the number sold column.
- Change the markup?
- Change the number ordered?

Save and print.

			COMPANY NAME				
			INVENTORY FOR MONTH OF ?				
	OUR	MARKUP	RETAIL	BEGIN	NUM	NUM	END
ITEM	COST	%	PRICE	INV	ORDER	SOLD	INV
PCD140							
DTS500							
HCD240							
SSS200							
MDC340							
STS400							
					COST OF		
					GOODS		GROSS
ITEM	PURCHASES		SALES		SOLD		PROFIT
PCD140							
DTS500							
HCD240							
SSS200							
MDC340							
STS400							
TOTALS	####		####		####		####

Job 21 continues on page 28

Task 3: Cash Flow Spreadsheet

Open **CASHFLOW** and copy the spreadsheet from July tab to August tab.

- Transfer Cash Balance for July to Cash from Previous Month for August
- Change Purchases?
- Change Advertising?
- Change Payroll Expense?
- Enter "zero" for Total Sales

Save and print.

	COMPANY NAME			
	CASH FLOW FOR MONTH OF ?			
Cash From Previous Month				
Purchases		####		
OPERATING EXPENSES:				
Advertising Expense				
Payroll Expense				
Rent Expense				
Market Research Expense	$ 200.00			
Interest Expense	$ 458.33			
Misc. Expense	$ 500.00			
Total Expenses		####		
Cash Before Sales			####	
Total Sales			INVENTRY SALES TOTAL	
Cash Balance			####	

Task 4: Monthly Audit Form

Open the **AUDTFORM** template and print. Complete the preliminary part of the Monthly Audit Form for August.

MONTHLY AUDIT FORM

MONTH: ____________________

COMPANY NAME:

____

INVENTORY

Product	Cost	Retail	Beginning Inventory	Number Order	Total Inventory	Number Sold	Ending Inventory
1. PCD140	________	________	________	________	________	________	________
2. DTS500	________	________	________	________	________	________	________
3. HCD240	________	________	________	________	________	________	________
4. SSS200	________	________	________	________	________	________	________
5. MDC340	________	________	________	________	________	________	________
6. STS400	________	________	________	________	________	________	________

CASH FLOW

Cash from Previous Month	____________________	
Purchases (minus)	____________________	-
Total Expenses (minus)	____________________	-
Cash Before Sales (equals)	____________________	=
Total Sales (plus)	____________________	+
Cash Balance (equals)	____________________	=

INCOME STATEMENT

Total Sales	____________________	
Cost of Goods Sold (minus)	____________________	-
Gross Profit (equals)	____________________	=
Total Expenses (minus)	____________________	-
Net Profit (equals)	____________________	=

Job 21 continues on page 30

Task 5: Data Input Form

Complete the Data Input Form for August.

Company Name: ______________________

DATA INPUT FORM

MONTH: July

Location $____________ Advertising $____________

Monthly Payroll $____________ Monthly Payroll Hours ____________

Product	Retail Price	Total Inventory
1. PCD140	________	________
2. DTS500	________	________
3. HCD240	________	________
4. SSS200	________	________
5. MDC340	________	________
6. STS400	________	________

MONTH: August

Location $____________ Advertising $____________

Monthly Payroll $____________ Monthly Payroll Hours ____________

Product	Retail Price	Total Inventory
1. PCD140	________	________
2. DTS500	________	________
3. HCD240	________	________
4. SSS200	________	________
5. MDC340	________	________
6. STS400	________	________

MONTH: September

Location $____________ Advertising Dollars $____________

Monthly Payroll $____________ Monthly Payroll Hours ____________

Product	Retail Price	Total Inventory
1. PCD140	________	________
2. DTS500	________	________
3. HCD240	________	________
4. SSS200	________	________
5. MDC340	________	________
6. STS400	________	________

Job 22
Computer Purchase Letter

Instructions:

Using your word processing software, open **J2LTHD** and save as **J22CMPLT.** Write a letter to your banker to secure a loan to purchase a computer system. Resave and print.

COMPUTER LETTER

You have recently discovered a great deal of paperwork that is involved in operating a business. A computer system is a must!, Write a letter to your banker (First Bank, Inc., 1000 State Street, Your City, State, ZIP) applying for a loan to purchase computer equipment for your business.

¶ 1: State the nature of the request--to apply for a loan of $???? (calculate the total amount needed) to purchase a computer system.

¶ 2: Describe **in very general terms** the hardware and software needed and explain the tasks for which the computer will be used (payroll, inventory, etc.).

¶ 3: Conclude your letter with a goodwill closing.

Use the following information:

BRAND:	Hewlett Packard
HARDWARE:	133 MHz Pentium processor; 16MB RAM 1.6 GB hard drive 1 MB video memory Six-speed CD-ROM drive 16-bit 3D sound and speakers 28.8 internal fax/modem w/voice mail Telephone answering system Microsoft Windows 95
PRICE:	$2299

BRAND:	Canon
HARDWARE:	Color Bubble Jet Printer
PRICE:	$299

SOFTWARE:	Microsoft Office
PRICE:	$499

Job 23
Finish August

Instructions:

Task 1: Update Inventory Spreadsheet

Open **INVENTRY**—August and enter the number sold from the results printout. Save and print.

			COMPANY NAME				
			INVENTORY FOR MONTH OF ?				
	OUR	MARKUP	RETAIL	BEGIN	NUM	NUM	END
ITEM	COST	%	PRICE	INV	ORDER	SOLD	INV
PCD140							
DTS500							
HCD240							
SSS200							
MDC340							
STS400							
					COST OF		
					GOODS		GROSS
ITEM	PURCHASES		SALES		SOLD		PROFIT
PCD140							
DTS500							
HCD240							
SSS200							
MDC340							
STS400							
TOTALS	####		####		####		####

Task 2: Update Cash Flow Spreadsheet

Open **CASHFLOW**—August and enter SALES TOTAL from the inventory spreadsheet. Save and print.

	COMPANY NAME			
	CASH FLOW FOR MONTH OF ?			
Cash From Previous Month				
Purchases		####		
OPERATING EXPENSES:				
Advertising Expense				
Payroll Expense				
Rent Expense				
Market Research Expense	$ 200.00			
Interest Expense	$ 458.33			
Misc. Expense	$ 500.00			
Total Expenses		####		
Cash Before Sales			####	
Total Sales			INVENTRY SALES TOTAL	
Cash Balance			####	

Task 3: Finalize Monthly Audit Form

Complete the Monthly Audit Form and compare those figures with the completed Cash Flow and Inventory Statement.

MONTHLY AUDIT FORM

MONTH: ____________________

COMPANY NAME:

____

INVENTORY

Product	Cost	Retail	Beginning Inventory	Number Order	Total Inventory	Number Sold	Ending Inventory
1. PCD140							
2. DTS500							
3. HCD240							
4. SSS200							
5. MDC340							
6. STS400							

CASH FLOW

Cash from Previous Month	____________	
Purchases (minus)	____________	-
Total Expenses (minus)	____________	-
Cash Before Sales (equals)	____________	=
Total Sales (plus)	____________	+
Cash Balance (equals)	____________	=

INCOME STATEMENT

Total Sales	____________	
Cost of Goods Sold (minus)	____________	-
Gross Profit (equals)	____________	=
Total Expenses (minus)	____________	-
Net Profit (equals)	____________	=

Job 23 continues on page 34

Task 4: Income Spreadsheet

Open **INCOMEST** and copy the spreadsheet from July tab to August tab. Make necessary changes for August such as:

- Change individual Revenue figures
- Change Cost of Goods Sold total
- Change Advertising Expense?
- Change Payroll Expense?

Information should be obtained from the inventory and cash flow spreadsheets.

Save and print.

	COMPANY NAME		
	INCOME STATEMENT FOR MONTH OF ?		
REVENUE:			
PCD140	INVENTRY SALES		
DTS500			
HCD240			
SSS200			
MDC340			
STS400			
TOTAL SALES		#####	
Cost of Goods Sold		INVENTRY TOTAL	
Gross Profit			#####
OPERATING EXPENSES:			
Advertising Expense	CASHFLOW		
Payroll Expense			
Rent Expense			
Market Research Exp.	$200.00		
Interest Expense	$458.33		
Misc. Expense	$500.00		
Total Expenses			#####
Net Profit/Loss			#####

Task 5: Pie & Bar Charts

Using the **INCOMEST**—August spreadsheet, create a bar (column) chart from the Revenue section. Create a pie chart from the Expense section. Save and print.

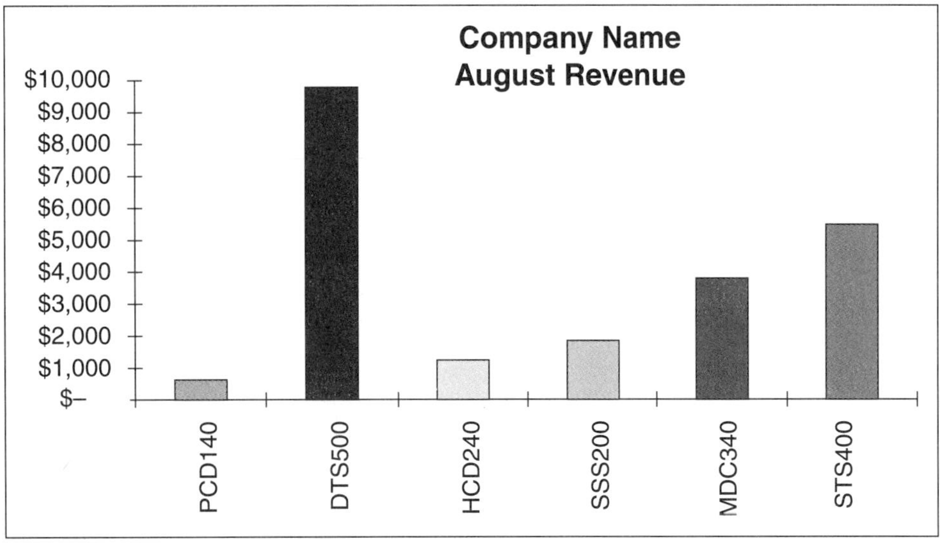

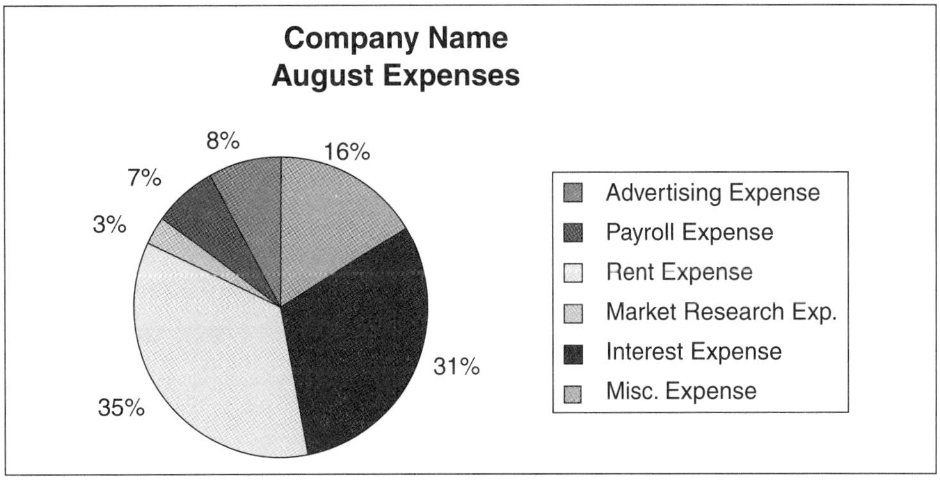

Job 24
Begin September

Instructions:

Task 1: Payroll Spreadsheet

Open **MPAYROLL** and copy the spreadsheet from August tab to September tab. Make decisions and changes for September such as:

- Change Hours Worked
- Hire or fire employee?

Save and print.

				COMPANY NAME									
				PAYROLL FOR MONTH OF ?									
								TOTAL	PAY	GROSS	WH	FICA	NET
EMPLOYEE	SUN	MON	TUE	WED	THUR	FRI	SAT	HOURS	RATE	PAY	TAX	TAX	PAY
Employee #1													
Employee #2								<40	($5.15-$6.25)				
Employee #3													
Employee #4													
WEEKLY TOTALS								####		####	####	####	####
MONTHLY TOTALS								####					####

Task 2: Inventory Spreadsheet

Open **INVENTRY** and copy the spreadsheet from August tab to September tab.

- Transfer Ending Inventory for August to Beginning Inventory for September
- Enter "zeros" in the number sold column
- Change the markup?
- Change the number ordered?

Save and print.

			COMPANY NAME				
			INVENTORY FOR MONTH OF ?				
	OUR	MARKUP	RETAIL	BEGIN	NUM	NUM	END
ITEM	COST	%	PRICE	INV	ORDER	SOLD	INV
PCD140							
DTS500							
HCD240							
SSS200							
MDC340							
STS400							
					COST OF		
					GOODS		GROSS
ITEM	PURCHASES		SALES		SOLD		PROFIT
PCD140							
DTS500							
HCD240							
SSS200							
MDC340							
STS400							
TOTALS	####		####		####		####

Task 3: Cash Flow Spreadsheet

Open **CASHFLOW** and copy the spreadsheet from August tab to September tab.

- Transfer Cash Balance for August to Cash from Previous Month for September
- Change Purchases?
- Change Advertising?
- Change Payroll Expense?
- Enter "zero" for Total Sales

Save and print.

	COMPANY NAME			
	CASH FLOW FOR MONTH OF ?			
Cash From Previous Month				
Purchases		####		
OPERATING EXPENSES:				
Advertising Expense				
Payroll Expense				
Rent Expense				
Market Research Expense	$ 200.00			
Interest Expense	$ 458.33			
Misc. Expense	$ 500.00			
Total Expenses		####		
Cash Before Sales			####	
Total Sales			INVENTRY SALES TOTAL	
Cash Balance			####	

Job 24 continues on page 38

Task 4: Monthly Audit Form

Open the **AUDTFORM** template and print. Complete the preliminary part of the Monthly Audit Form for September.

MONTHLY AUDIT FORM

MONTH: ________________

COMPANY NAME:

____

INVENTORY

Product	Cost	Retail	Beginning Inventory	Number Order	Total Inventory	Number Sold	Ending Inventory
1. PCD140							
2. DTS500							
3. HCD240							
4. SSS200							
5. MDC340							
6. STS400							

CASH FLOW

Cash from Previous Month	________________	
Purchases (minus)	________________	-
Total Expenses (minus)	________________	-
Cash Before Sales (equals)	________________	=
Total Sales (plus)	________________	+
Cash Balance (equals)	________________	=

INCOME STATEMENT

Total Sales	________________	
Cost of Goods Sold (minus)	________________	-
Gross Profit (equals)	________________	=
Total Expenses (minus)	________________	-
Net Profit (equals)	________________	=

Task 5: Data Input Form

Complete the Data Input Form for September.

Company Name: ______________________________

DATA INPUT FORM

MONTH: July

Location $________________ Advertising $________________

Monthly Payroll $____________ Monthly Payroll Hours ____________

Product	Retail Price	Total Inventory
1. PCD140	________	________
2. DTS500	________	________
3. HCD240	________	________
4. SSS200	________	________
5. MDC340	________	________
6. STS400	________	________

MONTH: August

Location $________________ Advertising $________________

Monthly Payroll $____________ Monthly Payroll Hours ____________

Product	Retail Price	Total Inventory
1. PCD140	________	________
2. DTS500	________	________
3. HCD240	________	________
4. SSS200	________	________
5. MDC340	________	________
6. STS400	________	________

MONTH: September

Location $________________ Advertising Dollars $____________

Monthly Payroll $____________ Monthly Payroll Hours ____________

Product	Retail Price	Total Inventory
1. PCD140	________	________
2. DTS500	________	________
3. HCD240	________	________
4. SSS200	________	________
5. MDC340	________	________
6. STS400	________	________

Job 25
Applicants Database

Instructions:

Task 1: Taking Applications

Using your database software, create a database file and save as **J25APPLC.**

PART-TIME APPLICANTS

TASK 1:

Your business is beginning to prosper and you are considering hiring additional part-time employees for the busy weekends. Using your database software, create a database file/table entering the information compiled from application forms. Use the fields and formatting data shown below. Enter the applicant records, print, and save the file/table as **J25APPLC.**

FIELD NAME	TYPE	SIZE
1) LAST	Text	12
2) FIRST	Text	12
3) PHONE	Text	12
4) EXP	Number	—
5) DAY	Text	3
6) #HRS	Number	—

LAST	FIRST	PHONE	EXP	DAY	# HRS
Jackson	Terry	893-4333	0	Sat	6
Crawley	Lee	444-0992	12	Sun	8
Smith	Shondra	466-3433	0	Sat	4
Hernandez	Enrique	893-4900	15	Sat	8
Murphy	Blake	444-2434	6	Sat	6
Johnson	Lou	469-5467	13	Sun	6
Brawley	Kevin	894-0921	20	Sun	8
Chan	May	466-5200	12	Sat	6
Tanner	Lucas	444-2998	24	Sun	6
Henderson	Tanner	894-2344	10	Sat	4
Johnson	Tina	893-9011	9	Sat	6
Garcia	Lupita	469-6399	14	Sun	8
Williams	Paul	469-2212	18	Sun	6
Kelly	David	893-4798	10	Sat	8
Butler	Devon	893-7323	8	Sun	8
Reynolds	Sampson	893-8210	0	Sat	6
Manning	Betsy	444-9232	7	Sat	4

Tasks 2–4: Sorting the Applicants

Using the **J25APPLC** file, use Query and Sort as indicated.

TASK 2:

A. Showing all fields, query the data to display all applicants with at least 12 months experience.

B. Sort the query results into descending order by EXP and ascending order by LAST.

C. Save query table as **12MO** and print.

TASK 3:

A. Showing all fields, query the data to display all applicants who can work (a) 6 or more hours on (b) Saturday.

B. Sort the query results into descending order by #HRS and ascending order by LAST.

C. Save query table as **SAT** and print.

TASK 4:

A. Showing all fields, query the data to display all applicants (a) with more than 6 months experience who can work on (b) Saturday OR Sunday.

B. Sort the query results into descending order by EXP.

C. Save query table as **SAT/SUN** and print.

Job 26
Finish September

Instructions:

Task 1: Update Inventory Spreadsheet

Open **INVENTRY**—September and enter the number sold from the results printout. Save and print.

			COMPANY NAME				
			INVENTORY FOR MONTH OF ?				
	OUR	MARKUP	RETAIL	BEGIN	NUM	NUM	END
ITEM	COST	%	PRICE	INV	ORDER	SOLD	INV
PCD140							
DTS500							
HCD240							
SSS200							
MDC340							
STS400							
					COST OF		
					GOODS		GROSS
ITEM	PURCHASES		SALES		SOLD		PROFIT
PCD140							
DTS500							
HCD240							
SSS200							
MDC340							
STS400							
TOTALS	####		####		####		####

Task 2: Update Cash Flow Spreadsheet

Open **CASHFLOW**—September and enter SALES TOTAL from the inventory spreadsheet. Save and print.

	COMPANY NAME			
	CASH FLOW FOR MONTH OF ?			
Cash From Previous Month				
Purchases		####		
OPERATING EXPENSES:				
Advertising Expense				
Payroll Expense				
Rent Expense				
Market Research Expense	$ 200.00			
Interest Expense	$ 458.33			
Misc. Expense	$ 500.00			
Total Expenses		####		
Cash Before Sales			####	
Total Sales			INVENTRY SALES TOTAL	
Cash Balance			####	

Task 3: Finalize Monthly Audit Form

Complete the Monthly Audit Form and compare those figures with the completed Cash Flow and Inventory Statement.

MONTHLY AUDIT FORM

MONTH: ________________

COMPANY NAME:

____

INVENTORY

Product	Cost	Retail	Beginning Inventory	Number Order	Total Inventory	Number Sold	Ending Inventory
1. PCD140							
2. DTS500							
3. HCD240							
4. SSS200							
5. MDC340							
6. STS400							

CASH FLOW

Cash from Previous Month	________________	
Purchases (minus)	________________	-
Total Expenses (minus)	________________	-
Cash Before Sales (equals)	________________	=
Total Sales (plus)	________________	+
Cash Balance (equals)	________________	=

INCOME STATEMENT

Total Sales	________________	
Cost of Goods Sold (minus)	________________	-
Gross Profit (equals)	________________	=
Total Expenses (minus)	________________	-
Net Profit (equals)	________________	=

Job 26 continues on page 44

Task 4: Income Spreadsheet

Open **INCOMEST** and copy the spreadsheet from August tab to September tab. Make necessary changes for September such as:

- Change individual Revenue figures
- Change Cost of Goods Sold total
- Change Advertising Expense?
- Change Payroll Expense?

Information should be obtained from the Inventory and Cash Flow spreadsheets.

Save and print.

	COMPANY NAME		
	INCOME STATEMENT FOR MONTH OF ?		
REVENUE:			
PCD140	INVENTRY SALES		
DTS500			
HCD240			
SSS200			
MDC340			
STS400			
TOTAL SALES		#####	
Cost of Goods Sold		INVENTRY TOTAL	
Gross Profit			#####
OPERATING EXPENSES:			
Advertising Expense	CASHFLOW		
Payroll Expense			
Rent Expense			
Market Research Exp.	$200.00		
Interest Expense	$458.33		
Misc. Expense	$500.00		
Total Expenses			#####
Net Profit/Loss			#####

Task 5: Pie & Bar Charts

Using the **INCOMEST**—September spreadsheet, create a bar (column) chart from the Revenue section. Create a pie chart from the Expense section. Save and print.

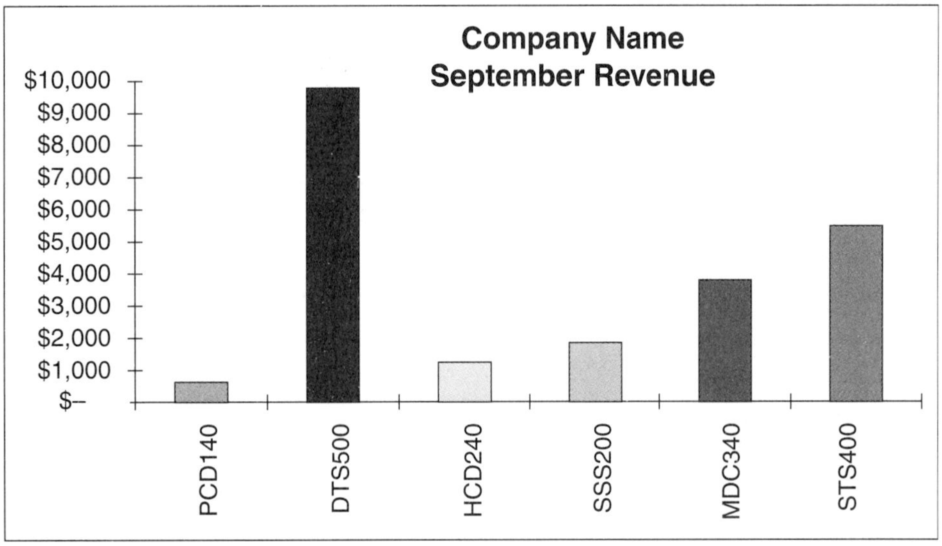

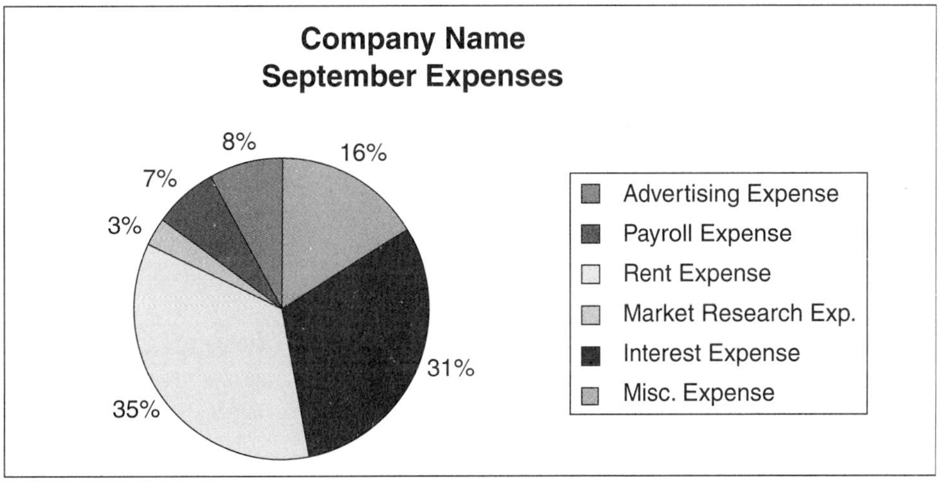

Job 27

Begin October

Instructions:

Task 1: Payroll Spreadsheet

Open **MPAYROLL** and copy the spreadsheet from September tab to October tab. Make decisions and changes for October such as:

- Change Hours Worked
- Change Rate of Pay?
- Hire or fire employee?

Save and print.

				COMPANY NAME									
				PAYROLL FOR MONTH OF ?									
EMPLOYEE	SUN	MON	TUE	WED	THUR	FRI	SAT	TOTAL HOURS	PAY RATE	GROSS PAY	WH TAX	FICA TAX	NET PAY
Employee #1													
Employee #2								<40	($5.15-$6.25)				
Employee #3													
Employee #4													
WEEKLY TOTALS								####		####	####	####	####
MONTHLY TOTALS								####					####

Task 2: Inventory Spreadsheet

Open **INVENTRY** and copy the spreadsheet from September tab to October tab.

- Transfer Ending Inventory for September to Beginning Inventory for October
- Enter "zeros" in the number sold column
- Change the markup?
- Change the number ordered?

Save and print.

			COMPANY NAME				
			INVENTORY FOR MONTH OF ?				
ITEM	OUR COST	MARKUP %	RETAIL PRICE	BEGIN INV	NUM ORDER	NUM SOLD	END INV
PCD140							
DTS500							
HCD240							
SSS200							
MDC340							
STS400							
ITEM	PURCHASES		SALES		COST OF GOODS SOLD		GROSS PROFIT
PCD140							
DTS500							
HCD240							
SSS200							
MDC340							
STS400							
TOTALS	####		####		####		####

Task 3: Cash Flow Spreadsheet

Open **CASHFLOW** and copy the spreadsheet from September tab to October tab.

- Transfer Cash Balance for September to Cash from Previous Month for October
- Change Purchases?
- Change Advertising?
- Change Payroll Expense?
- Enter "zero" for Total Sales

Save and print.

	COMPANY NAME			
	CASH FLOW FOR MONTH OF ?			
Cash From Previous Month				
Purchases		####		
OPERATING EXPENSES:				
Advertising Expense				
Payroll Expense				
Rent Expense				
Market Research Expense	$ 200.00			
Interest Expense	$ 458.33			
Misc. Expense	$ 500.00			
Total Expenses		####		
Cash Before Sales			####	
Total Sales			INVENTRY SALES TOTAL	
Cash Balance			####	

Job 27 continues on page 48

Task 4: Monthly Audit Form

Open the **AUDTFORM** template and print. Complete the preliminary part of the Monthly Audit Form for October.

MONTHLY AUDIT FORM

MONTH: ____________________

COMPANY NAME:

____

INVENTORY

Product	Cost	Retail	Beginning Inventory	Number Order	Total Inventory	Number Sold	Ending Inventory
1. PCD140	________	________	________	________	________	________	________
2. DTS500	________	________	________	________	________	________	________
3. HCD240	________	________	________	________	________	________	________
4. SSS200	________	________	________	________	________	________	________
5. MDC340	________	________	________	________	________	________	________
6. STS400	________	________	________	________	________	________	________

CASH FLOW

Cash from Previous Month	____________________	
Purchases (minus)	____________________	-
Total Expenses (minus)	____________________	-
Cash Before Sales (equals)	____________________	=
Total Sales (plus)	____________________	+
Cash Balance (equals)	____________________	=

INCOME STATEMENT

Total Sales	____________________	
Cost of Goods Sold (minus)	____________________	-
Gross Profit (equals)	____________________	=
Total Expenses (minus)	____________________	-
Net Profit (equals)	____________________	=

Task 5: Data Input Form

Complete the Data Input Form for October.

Company Name: ______________________

DATA INPUT FORM

MONTH: October

Location $__________ Advertising $__________

Monthly Payroll $__________ Monthly Payroll Hours __________

Product	Retail Price	Total Inventory
1. PCD140	________	________
2. DTS500	________	________
3. HCD240	________	________
4. SSS200	________	________
5. MDC340	________	________
6. STS400	________	________

MONTH: November

Location $__________ Advertising $__________

Monthly Payroll $__________ Monthly Payroll Hours __________

Product	Retail Price	Total Inventory
1. PCD140	________	________
2. DTS500	________	________
3. HCD240	________	________
4. SSS200	________	________
5. MDC340	________	________
6. STS400	________	________

MONTH: December

Location $__________ Advertising Dollars $__________

Monthly Payroll $__________ Monthly Payroll Hours __________

Product	Retail Price	Total Inventory
1. PCD140	________	________
2. DTS500	________	________
3. HCD240	________	________
4. SSS200	________	________
5. MDC340	________	________
6. STS400	________	________

Job 28
Customer Letter

Instructions:

Using your word processing software, open **J2LTHD** and save as **J28CSTLT.** Write a goodwill letter to an unhappy customer. Follow the example as a guideline. Resave and print.

CUSTOMER LETTER

You have just received a letter from a customer stating that when he visited your store, he waited ten minutes for service because the only available salesperson was talking on the telephone. In addition, this salesperson was not able to provide adequate information about the merchandise. Consequently, this frustrated customer left your store without making a purchase.

Write a goodwill letter thanking the customer for bringing the problems to your attention. Include an explanation of what is being done to correct the problems, and encourage this customer to return to your store. Remember, a satisfied customer means future business!

Current Date

Mr. Richard Crabtree
7610 Knoxville Ave.
Your City, ST ZIP

Dear Mr. Crabtree:

¶ 1: Thank the customer for bringing the situation to your attention and acknowledge the problems.

¶ 2: Provide details explaining what is being done to correct the problems.

¶ 3: Provide a goodwill closing, coupon, or incentive to get customer to return to the store.

Sincerely yours,

Xxxxxx Xxxxxx
General Manager

Job 29
Finish October

Instructions:

Task 1: Update Inventory Spreadsheet

Open **INVENTRY**—October and enter the number sold from the results printout. Save and print.

			COMPANY NAME				
			INVENTORY FOR MONTH OF ?				
	OUR	MARKUP	RETAIL	BEGIN	NUM	NUM	END
ITEM	COST	%	PRICE	INV	ORDER	SOLD	INV
PCD140							
DTS500							
HCD240							
SSS200							
MDC340							
STS400							
					COST OF		
					GOODS		GROSS
ITEM	PURCHASES		SALES		SOLD		PROFIT
PCD140							
DTS500							
HCD240							
SSS200							
MDC340							
STS400							
TOTALS	####		####		####		####

Task 2: Update Cash Flow Spreadsheet

Open **CASHFLOW**—October and enter SALES TOTAL from the inventory spreadsheet. Save and print.

	COMPANY NAME			
	CASH FLOW FOR MONTH OF ?			
Cash From Previous Month				
Purchases		####		
OPERATING EXPENSES:				
Advertising Expense				
Payroll Expense				
Rent Expense				
Market Research Expense	$ 200.00			
Interest Expense	$ 458.33			
Misc. Expense	$ 500.00			
Total Expenses		####		
Cash Before Sales			####	
Total Sales			INVENTRY SALES TOTAL	
Cash Balance			####	

Job 29 continues on page 52

Task 3: Finalize Monthly Audit Form

Complete the Monthly Audit Form and compare those figures with the completed Cash Flow and Inventory Statement.

MONTHLY AUDIT FORM

MONTH: ____________________

COMPANY NAME:

____

INVENTORY

Product	Cost	Retail	Beginning Inventory	Number Order	Total Inventory	Number Sold	Ending Inventory
1. PCD140							
2. DTS500							
3. HCD240							
4. SSS200							
5. MDC340							
6. STS400							

CASH FLOW

Cash from Previous Month	____________	
Purchases (minus)	____________	-
Total Expenses (minus)	____________	-
Cash Before Sales (equals)	____________	=
Total Sales (plus)	____________	+
Cash Balance (equals)	____________	=

INCOME STATEMENT

Total Sales	____________	
Cost of Goods Sold (minus)	____________	-
Gross Profit (equals)	____________	=
Total Expenses (minus)	____________	-
Net Profit (equals)	____________	=

Task 4: Income Spreadsheet

Open **INCOMEST** and copy the spreadsheet from September tab to October tab. Make necessary changes for October such as:

- Change individual Revenue figures
- Change Cost of Goods Sold total
- Change Advertising Expense?
- Change Payroll Expense?

Information should be obtained from the inventory and cash flow spreadsheets.

Save and print.

	COMPANY NAME		
INCOME STATEMENT FOR MONTH OF ?			
REVENUE:			
PCD140	INVENTRY SALES		
DTS500			
HCD240			
SSS200			
MDC340			
STS400			
TOTAL SALES		#####	
Cost of Goods Sold		INVENTRY TOTAL	
Gross Profit			#####
OPERATING EXPENSES:			
Advertising Expense	CASHFLOW		
Payroll Expense			
Rent Expense			
Market Research Exp.	$200.00		
Interest Expense	$458.33		
Misc. Expense	$500.00		
Total Expenses			#####
Net Profit/Loss			#####

Job 29 continues on page 54

Task 5: Pie & Bar Charts

Using the **INCOMEST—** October spreadsheet, create a bar (column) chart from the Revenue section. Create a pie chart from the Expense section. Save and print.

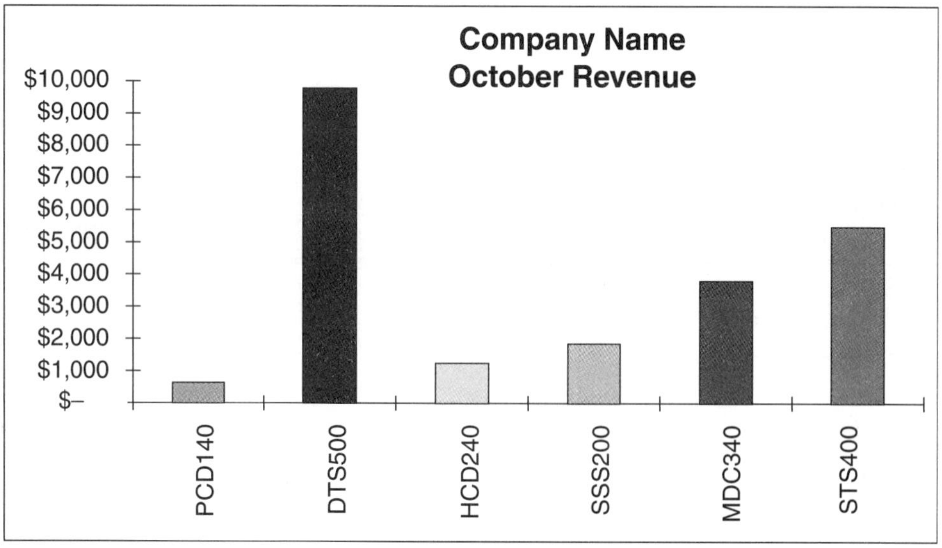

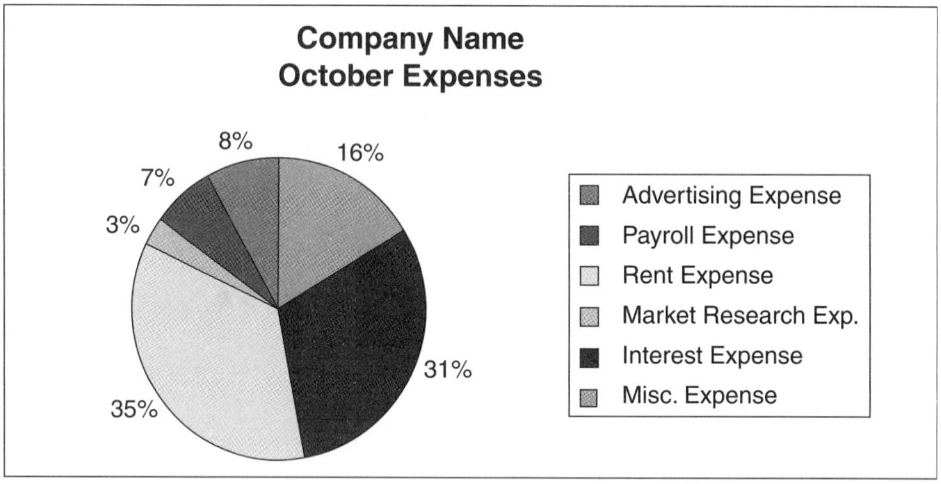

Job 30
Begin November

Instructions:

Task 1: Payroll Spreadsheet

Open **MPAYROLL** and copy the spreadsheet from October tab to November tab. Make decisions and changes for November such as:

- Change Hours Worked
- Change Rate of Pay?
- Hire or fire employee?

Save and print.

EMPLOYEE	SUN	MON	TUE	WED	THUR	FRI	SAT	TOTAL HOURS	PAY RATE	GROSS PAY	WH TAX	FICA TAX	NET PAY
			COMPANY NAME PAYROLL FOR MONTH OF ?										
Employee #1													
Employee #2								<40	($5.15-$6.25)				
Employee #3													
Employee #4													
WEEKLY TOTALS								####		####	####	####	####
MONTHLY TOTALS								####					####

Task 2: Inventory Spreadsheet

Open **INVENTRY** and copy the spreadsheet from October tab to November tab.

- Transfer Ending Inventory for October to Beginning Inventory for November
- Enter "zeros" in the number sold column
- Change the markup?
- Change the number ordered?

Save and print.

ITEM	OUR COST	MARKUP %	RETAIL PRICE	BEGIN INV	NUM ORDER	NUM SOLD	END INV
			COMPANY NAME INVENTORY FOR MONTH OF ?				
PCD140							
DTS500							
HCD240							
SSS200							
MDC340							
STS400							
ITEM	PURCHASES		SALES		COST OF GOODS SOLD		GROSS PROFIT
PCD140							
DTS500							
HCD240							
SSS200							
MDC340							
STS400							
TOTALS	####		####		####		####

Job 30 continues on page 56

Task 3: Cash Flow Spreadsheet

Open **CASHFLOW** and copy the spreadsheet from October tab to November tab.

- Transfer Cash Balance for October to Cash from Previous Month for November
- Change Purchases?
- Change Advertising?
- Change Payroll Expense?
- Enter "zero" for Total Sales

Save and print.

	COMPANY NAME			
	CASH FLOW FOR MONTH OF ?			
Cash From Previous Month				
Purchases		####		
OPERATING EXPENSES:				
Advertising Expense				
Payroll Expense				
Rent Expense				
Market Research Expense	$ 200.00			
Interest Expense	$ 458.33			
Misc. Expense	$ 500.00			
Total Expenses		####		
Cash Before Sales			####	
Total Sales			INVENTRY SALES TOTAL	
Cash Balance			####	

Task 4: Monthly Audit Form

Open the **AUDTFORM** template and print. Complete the preliminary part of the Monthly Audit Form for November.

MONTHLY AUDIT FORM

MONTH: ____________________

COMPANY NAME:

____

INVENTORY

Product	Cost	Retail	Beginning Inventory	Number Order	Total Inventory	Number Sold	Ending Inventory
1. PCD140							
2. DTS500							
3. HCD240							
4. SSS200							
5. MDC340							
6. STS400							

CASH FLOW

Cash from Previous Month	____________	
Purchases (minus)	____________	-
Total Expenses (minus)	____________	-
Cash Before Sales (equals)	____________	=
Total Sales (plus)	____________	+
Cash Balance (equals)	____________	=

INCOME STATEMENT

Total Sales	____________	
Cost of Goods Sold (minus)	____________	-
Gross Profit (equals)	____________	=
Total Expenses (minus)	____________	-
Net Profit (equals)	____________	=

Job 30 continues on page 58

Task 5: Data Input Form

Complete the Data Input Form for November.

Company Name: ______________________________

DATA INPUT FORM

MONTH: October

Location $__________________ Advertising $____________________

Monthly Payroll $______________ Monthly Payroll Hours ____________

Product	Retail Price	Total Inventory
1. PCD140	____________	____________
2. DTS500	____________	____________
3. HCD240	____________	____________
4. SSS200	____________	____________
5. MDC340	____________	____________
6. STS400	____________	____________

MONTH: November

Location $__________________ Advertising $____________________

Monthly Payroll $______________ Monthly Payroll Hours ____________

Product	Retail Price	Total Inventory
1. PCD140	____________	____________
2. DTS500	____________	____________
3. HCD240	____________	____________
4. SSS200	____________	____________
5. MDC340	____________	____________
6. STS400	____________	____________

MONTH: December

Location $__________________ Advertising Dollars $______________

Monthly Payroll $______________ Monthly Payroll Hours ____________

Product	Retail Price	Total Inventory
1. PCD140	____________	____________
2. DTS500	____________	____________
3. HCD240	____________	____________
4. SSS200	____________	____________
5. MDC340	____________	____________
6. STS400	____________	____________

Job 31
Presentation Graphics Slide Show

Instructions:

Using your presentation graphics software, create a slide show with seven slides following the guidelines. Save as **J31SLPRS** and print.

SLIDE PRESENTATION

To assist your customers during your busiest hours, use your presentation graphics software to create a slide show that will run continuously on your computer for easy customer referral.

1. The title slide should contain
   (a) your company name, address, and telephone number
   (b) your store hours (use a smaller font)
   (c) an appropriate graphic

2. Create an individual slide for *each* of your six products. Each slide should contain
   (a) the complete product name and stock number
   (b) a detailed description (refer to Product Description page)
   (c) your most current price
   (c) an appropriate graphic

3. The slide show should
   (a) run continuously
   (b) advance slides automatically after 15 seconds
   (c) have an appropriate **transition/effect** (i.e. fade) between slides

---

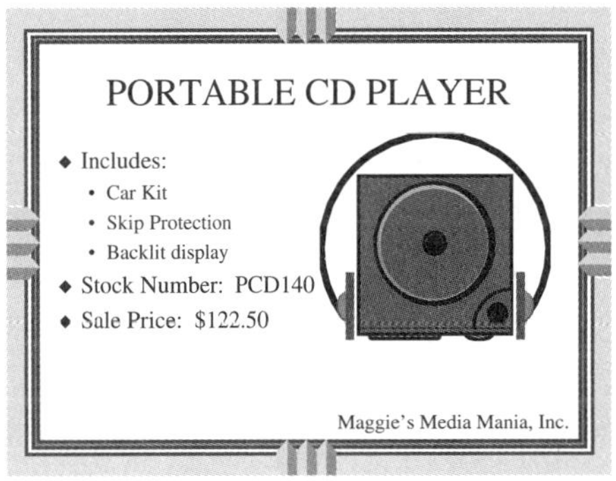

Job 32
Finish November

Instructions:

Task 1: Update Inventory Spreadsheet

Open **INVENTRY**—November and enter the number sold from the results printout. Save and print.

			COMPANY NAME				
			INVENTORY FOR MONTH OF ?				
	OUR	MARKUP	RETAIL	BEGIN	NUM	NUM	END
ITEM	COST	%	PRICE	INV	ORDER	SOLD	INV
PCD140							
DTS500							
HCD240							
SSS200							
MDC340							
STS400							
					COST OF		
					GOODS		GROSS
ITEM	PURCHASES		SALES		SOLD		PROFIT
PCD140							
DTS500							
HCD240							
SSS200							
MDC340							
STS400							
TOTALS	####		####		####		####

Task 2: Update Cash Flow Spreadsheet

Open **CASHFLOW**—November and enter SALES TOTAL from the inventory spreadsheet. Save and print.

	COMPANY NAME			
	CASH FLOW FOR MONTH OF ?			
Cash From Previous Month				
Purchases		####		
OPERATING EXPENSES:				
Advertising Expense				
Payroll Expense				
Rent Expense				
Market Research Expense	$ 200.00			
Interest Expense	$ 458.33			
Misc. Expense	$ 500.00			
Total Expenses		####		
Cash Before Sales			####	
Total Sales			INVENTRY SALES TOTAL	
Cash Balance			####	

Task 3: Finalize Monthly Audit Form

Complete the Monthly Audit Form and compare those figures with the completed Cash Flow and Inventory Statement.

MONTHLY AUDIT FORM

MONTH: ____________

COMPANY NAME: ________________________

INVENTORY

Product	Cost	Retail	Beginning Inventory	Number Order	Total Inventory	Number Sold	Ending Inventory
1. PCD140							
2. DTS500							
3. HCD240							
4. SSS200							
5. MDC340							
6. STS400							

CASH FLOW

Cash from Previous Month	____________	
Purchases (minus)	____________	-
Total Expenses (minus)	____________	-
Cash Before Sales (equals)	____________	=
Total Sales (plus)	____________	+
Cash Balance (equals)	____________	=

INCOME STATEMENT

Total Sales	____________	
Cost of Goods Sold (minus)	____________	-
Gross Profit (equals)	____________	=
Total Expenses (minus)	____________	-
Net Profit (equals)	____________	=

Job 32 continues on page 62

Task 4: Income Spreadsheet

Open **INCOMEST** and copy the spreadsheet from October tab to November tab. Make necessary changes for November such as:

- Change individual Revenue figures
- Change Cost of Goods Sold total
- Change Advertising expense?
- Change Payroll expense?

Information should be obtained from the inventory and cash flow spreadsheets.

Save and print.

	COMPANY NAME		
INCOME STATEMENT FOR MONTH OF ?			
REVENUE:			
PCD140	INVENTRY SALES		
DTS500			
HCD240			
SSS200			
MDC340			
STS400			
TOTAL SALES		#####	
Cost of Goods Sold		INVENTRY TOTAL	
Gross Profit			#####
OPERATING EXPENSES:			
Advertising Expense	CASHFLOW		
Payroll Expense			
Rent Expense			
Market Research Exp.	$200.00		
Interest Expense	$458.33		
Misc. Expense	$500.00		
Total Expenses			#####
Net Profit/Loss			#####

Task 5: Pie & Bar Charts

Using the **INCOMEST—**November spreadsheet, create a bar (column) chart from the Revenue section. Create a pie chart from the Expense section. Save and print.

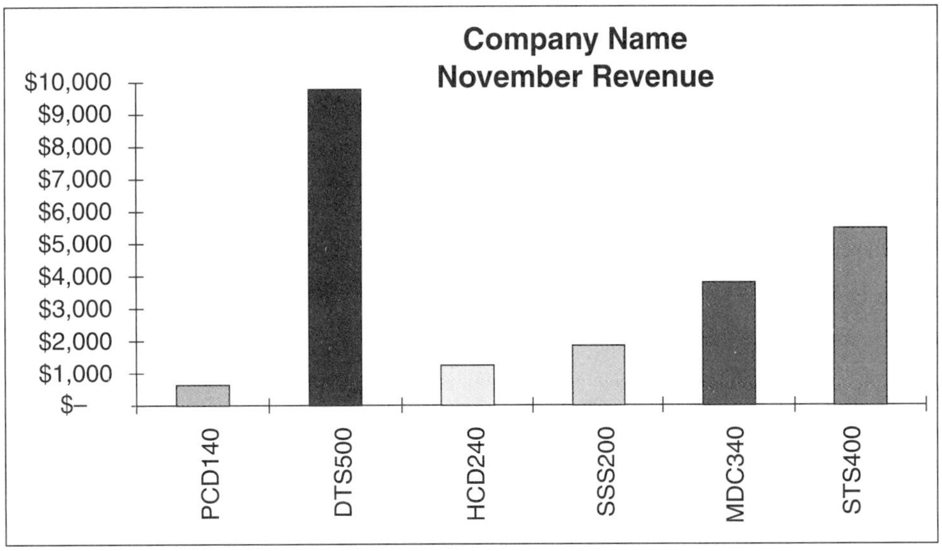

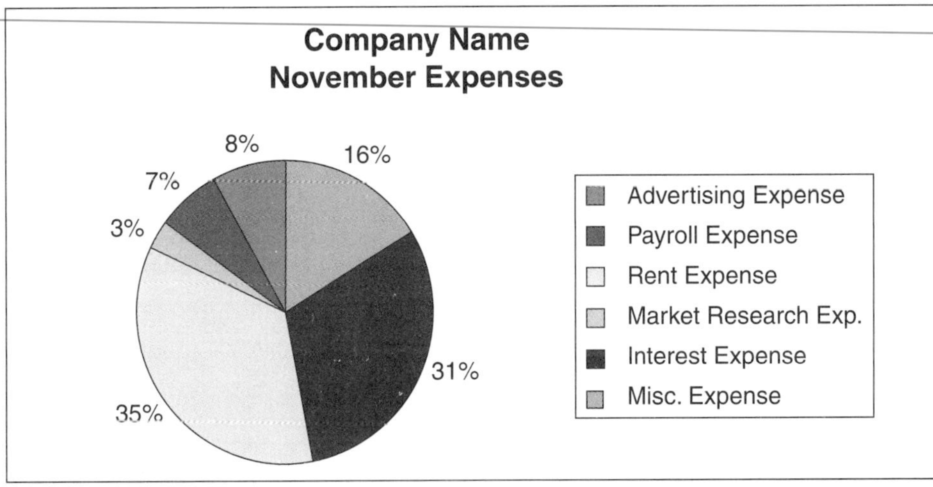

Job 33
Begin December

Instructions:

Task 1: Payroll Spreadsheet

Open **MPAYROLL** and copy the spreadsheet from November tab to December tab. Make decisions and changes for December such as:

- Change Hours Worked
- Change Rate of Pay?
- Hire or fire employee?

Save and print.

				COMPANY NAME PAYROLL FOR MONTH OF ?									
EMPLOYEE	SUN	MON	TUE	WED	THUR	FRI	SAT	TOTAL HOURS	PAY RATE	GROSS PAY	WH TAX	FICA TAX	NET PAY
Employee #1													
Employee #2								<40	($5.15-$6.25)				
Employee #3													
Employee #4													
WEEKLY TOTALS								####		####	####	####	####
MONTHLY TOTALS								####					####

Task 2: Inventory Spreadsheet

Open **INVENTRY** and copy the spreadsheet from November tab to December tab.

- Transfer Ending Inventory for November to Beginning Inventory for December
- Enter "zeros" in the number sold column
- Change the markup?
- Change the number ordered?

Save and print.

			COMPANY NAME INVENTORY FOR MONTH OF ?				
ITEM	OUR COST	MARKUP %	RETAIL PRICE	BEGIN INV	NUM ORDER	NUM SOLD	END INV
PCD140							
DTS500							
HCD240							
SSS200							
MDC340							
STS400							
ITEM	PURCHASES		SALES		COST OF GOODS SOLD		GROSS PROFIT
PCD140							
DTS500							
HCD240							
SSS200							
MDC340							
STS400							
TOTALS	####		####		####		####

Task 3: Cash Flow Spreadsheet

Open **CASHFLOW** and copy the spreadsheet from November tab to December tab.

- Transfer Cash Balance for November to Cash from Previous Month for December
- Change Purchases?
- Change Advertising?
- Change Payroll Expense?
- Enter "zero" for Total Sales

Save and print.

	COMPANY NAME			
	CASH FLOW FOR MONTH OF ?			
Cash From Previous Month				
Purchases		####		
OPERATING EXPENSES:				
Advertising Expense				
Payroll Expense				
Rent Expense				
Market Research Expense	$ 200.00			
Interest Expense	$ 458.33			
Misc. Expense	$ 500.00			
Total Expenses		####		
Cash Before Sales			####	
Total Sales			INVENTRY SALES TOTAL	
Cash Balance			####	

Job 33 continues on page 66

Task 4: Monthly Audit Form

Open the **AUDTFORM** template and print. Complete the preliminary part of the Monthly Audit Form for December.

MONTHLY AUDIT FORM

MONTH: ____________________

COMPANY NAME:

____

INVENTORY

Product	Cost	Retail	Beginning Inventory	Number Order	Total Inventory	Number Sold	Ending Inventory
1. PCD140							
2. DTS500							
3. HCD240							
4. SSS200							
5. MDC340							
6. STS400							

CASH FLOW

Cash from Previous Month	____________	
Purchases (minus)	____________	-
Total Expenses (minus)	____________	-
Cash Before Sales (equals)	____________	=
Total Sales (plus)	____________	+
Cash Balance (equals)	____________	=

INCOME STATEMENT

Total Sales	____________	
Cost of Goods Sold (minus)	____________	-
Gross Profit (equals)	____________	=
Total Expenses (minus)	____________	-
Net Profit (equals)	____________	=

Task 5: Data Input Form

Complete the Data Input Form for December.

Company Name: ______________________

DATA INPUT FORM

MONTH: October

Location $____________ Advertising $____________

Monthly Payroll $____________ Monthly Payroll Hours ____________

Product	Retail Price	Total Inventory
1. PCD140	________	________
2. DTS500	________	________
3. HCD240	________	________
4. SSS200	________	________
5. MDC340	________	________
6. STS400	________	________

MONTH: November

Location $____________ Advertising $____________

Monthly Payroll $____________ Monthly Payroll Hours ____________

Product	Retail Price	Total Inventory
1. PCD140	________	________
2. DTS500	________	________
3. HCD240	________	________
4. SSS200	________	________
5. MDC340	________	________
6. STS400	________	________

MONTH: December

Location $____________ Advertising Dollars $____________

Monthly Payroll $____________ Monthly Payroll Hours ____________

Product	Retail Price	Total Inventory
1. PCD140	________	________
2. DTS500	________	________
3. HCD240	________	________
4. SSS200	________	________
5. MDC340	________	________
6. STS400	________	________

Job 34
Mail Merge

Instructions:

Task 1: Main/Form Document

Using your word processing software, open **J2LTHD** and save as **J34MAIL.** Create the main/form document containing the letter.

MAIL MERGE

To enhance customer relations, many businesses send a letter to their customers thanking them for their business. Send a "thank you" letter to each of your customers who made a purchase in November.

TASK 1:

1. Using your word processing software, create the main/form document containing the text and the **merge codes**.
2. Use block letter style; begin the date 2.5" from the top. Save the letter as **J34MAIL.**

December 15, 199-

Title First Last
Address
City, State Postal Code

Dear **Title Last**:

Thank you for purchasing a **Product** from our store. Serving you has been a real pleasure.

As you know, your new **Product** is guaranteed for one year from the date of purchase. We are confident that it will perform up to your expectations. In the unlikely event that a problem should develop, please let us know at once. We will be glad to correct the situation.

Once again, thank you for selecting us for your home entertainment equipment. We look forward to serving you in the future.

Sincerely,

Your Name
General Manager

Task 2: Data Source/Data File

Using your word processing or database software, create the merge field names and data. Save as **J34MERGE** and print.

Task 3: Merge the Letter and Data

Using your word processing software, perform the merge and create the final letters. Save as **J34LETTR** and print.

TASK 2:

1. Create a data source/data file document using the following **merge field names** and data. Save as **J34MERGE.**

DATA SOURCE/DATA FILE

Title	*First*	*Last*	*Address*	*City*	*State*	*Postal Code*	*Product*
Mr.	Don	White	8181 Evergreen	Houston	TX	77045	DTS500
Ms.	Michelle	Corrigan	7602 Mosswood	Pasadena	TX	77428	HCD240
Dr.	Keith	Wong	5123 Prairie Creek	Tomball	TX	77773	DTS500
Mr.	Juan	Valdez	12648 Copper Mill	Houston	TX	77090	STS400

TASK 3:

1. Merge the main/form document with the data source/data file document.
2. Scroll through the new merged document, checking for merge errors.
3. Save the merged letters under a new document name, **J34LETTR**.
4. Print the resulting document (one copy of each merged letter).

NOTE: *Depending on your word processing software, the order of Tasks 1 and 2 may be reversed. If your database software is compatible with your word processing software, the customer names could be entered in a database table and then merged with the main/form document.*

Job 35

Finish December

Instructions:

Task 1: Update Inventory Spreadsheet

Open **INVENTRY—** December and enter the number sold from the results printout. Save and print.

			COMPANY NAME				
			INVENTORY FOR MONTH OF ?				
ITEM	OUR COST	MARKUP %	RETAIL PRICE	BEGIN INV	NUM ORDER	NUM SOLD	END INV
PCD140							
DTS500							
HCD240							
SSS200							
MDC340							
STS400							
ITEM	PURCHASES		SALES		COST OF GOODS SOLD		GROSS PROFIT
PCD140							
DTS500							
HCD240							
SSS200							
MDC340							
STS400							
TOTALS	####		####		####		####

Task 2: Update Cash Flow Spreadsheet

Open **CASHFLOW—** December and enter SALES TOTAL from the inventory spreadsheet. Save and print.

	COMPANY NAME			
	CASH FLOW FOR MONTH OF ?			
Cash From Previous Month				
Purchases		####		
OPERATING EXPENSES:				
Advertising Expense				
Payroll Expense				
Rent Expense				
Market Research Expense	$ 200.00			
Interest Expense	$ 458.33			
Misc. Expense	$ 500.00			
Total Expenses		####		
Cash Before Sales			####	
Total Sales			INVENTRY SALES TOTAL	
Cash Balance			####	

Task 3: Finalize Monthly Audit Form

Complete the Monthly Audit Form and compare those figures with the completed Cash Flow and Inventory Statement.

MONTHLY AUDIT FORM

MONTH: ____________________

COMPANY NAME:

____

INVENTORY

Product	Cost	Retail	Beginning Inventory	Number Order	Total Inventory	Number Sold	Ending Inventory
1. PCD140							
2. DTS500							
3. HCD240							
4. SSS200							
5. MDC340							
6. STS400							

CASH FLOW

Cash from Previous Month	____________________	
Purchases (minus)	____________________	-
Total Expenses (minus)	____________________	-
Cash Before Sales (equals)	____________________	=
Total Sales (plus)	____________________	+
Cash Balance (equals)	____________________	=

INCOME STATEMENT

Total Sales	____________________	
Cost of Goods Sold (minus)	____________________	-
Gross Profit (equals)	____________________	=
Total Expenses (minus)	____________________	-
Net Profit (equals)	____________________	=

Job 35 continues on page 72

Task 4: Income Spreadsheet

Open **INCOMEST** and copy the spreadsheet from November tab to December tab. Make necessary changes for December such as:

- Change individual Revenue figures
- Change Cost of Goods Sold total
- Change Advertising Expense?
- Change Payroll Expense?

Information should be obtained from the inventory and cash flow spreadsheets.

Save and print.

	COMPANY NAME		
INCOME STATEMENT FOR MONTH OF ?			
REVENUE:			
PCD140	INVENTRY SALES		
DTS500			
HCD240			
SSS200			
MDC340			
STS400			
TOTAL SALES		#####	
Cost of Goods Sold		INVENTRY TOTAL	
Gross Profit			#####
OPERATING EXPENSES:			
Advertising Expense	CASHFLOW		
Payroll Expense			
Rent Expense			
Market Research Exp.	$200.00		
Interest Expense	$458.33		
Misc. Expense	$500.00		
Total Expenses			#####
Net Profit/Loss			#####

Task 5: Pie & Bar Charts

Using the **INCOMEST**—December spreadsheet, create a bar (column) chart from the Revenue section. Create a pie chart from the Expense section. Save and print.

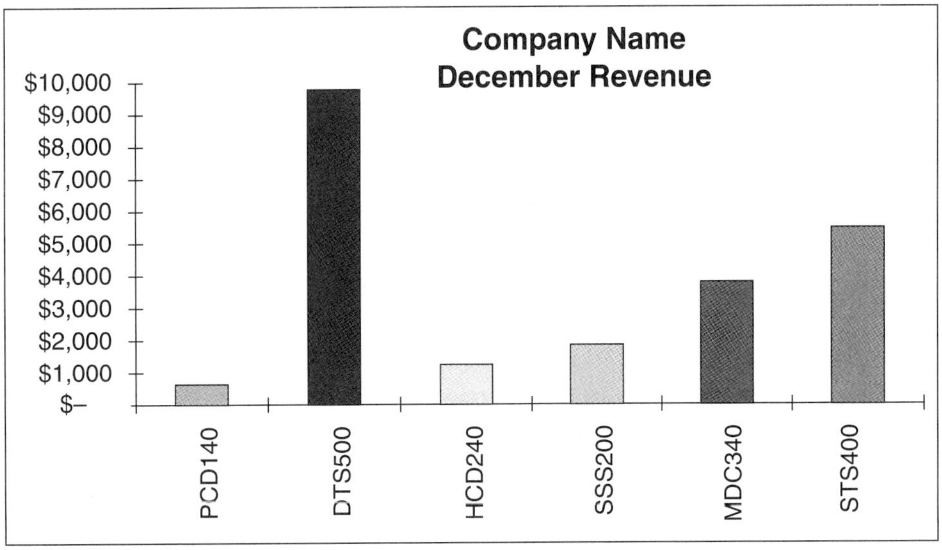

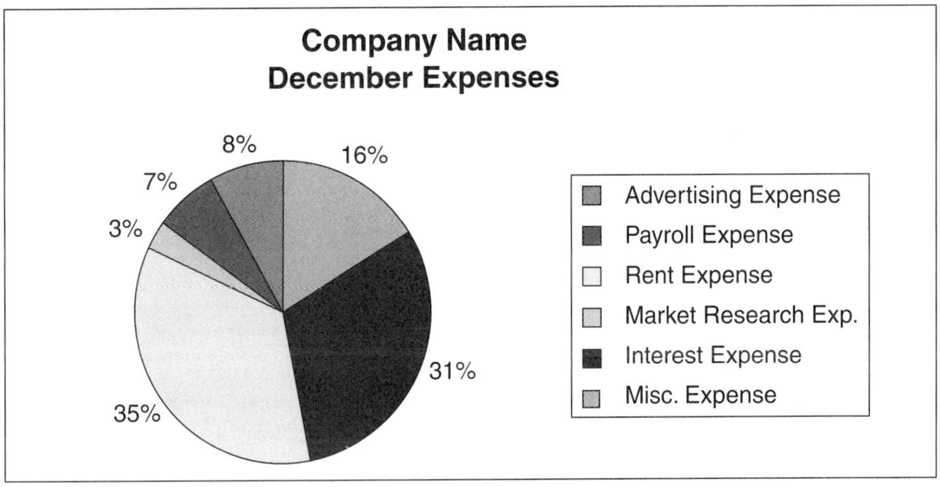

Job 36
Business Liquidation

Instructions:

Task 1: Sell Inventory

Open **INVENTRY—**December. Follow the instructions. Save and print.

BUSINESS LIQUIDATION

You have reached the end of your six month business commitment. While you have enjoyed owning and operating your own business, you have been offered a better opportunity with another company. Therefore, it is necessary to liquidate the inventory and dissolve your business.

TASK 1: GOING OUT OF BUSINESS SALE

Open the **INVENTRY--December** spreadsheet and sell all equipment at the COST price to liquidate inventory. Add column label and formula as shown:

LIQUIDATE INVENTORY: Our Cost * Ending Inventory

COMPANY NAME

INVENTORY FOR MONTH OF ?

ITEM	OUR COST	MARKUP %	RETAIL PRICE	BEGIN INV	NUM ORDER	NUM SOLD	END INV
PCD140							
DTS500							
HCD240							
SSS200							
MDC340							
STS400							

ITEM	PURCHASES		SALES	COST OF GOODS SOLD	GROSS PROFIT		LIQUIDATE INVENTORY
PCD140							(Our Cost * End INV)
DTS500							
HCD240							
SSS200							
MDC340							
STS400							
TOTALS	####		####	####	####		####

Task 2: Finalize Cash Flow

Open **CASHFLOW—December**. Follow the instructions. Save and print.

Terms:
Liquidate

TASK 2: FINALIZE CASH FLOW

Open the **CASHFLOW--December** spreadsheet and follow the instructions below: (1) Deposit "liquidation" sales and (2) pay back loan principal to bank. Add labels and formulas as shown:

LIQUIDATE INVENTORY:	Enter total amount calculated on INVENTRY
TOTAL CASH FOR 6 MONTHS:	Cash Balance + Liquidate Inventory
LOAN PAYOFFS:	$50,000 + (Computer loan amount)
FINAL CASH BALANCE:	Total Cash for 6 months - Loan payoffs

COMPANY NAME
CASH FLOW FOR MONTH OF ?

Cash From Previous Month			
Purchases		####	
OPERATING EXPENSES:			
Advertising Expense			
Payroll Expense			
Rent Expense			
Market Research Expense	$ 200.00		
Interest Expense	$ 458.33		
Misc. Expense	$ 500.00		
Total Expenses		####	
Cash Before Sales			####
Total Sales			INVENTRY SALES TOTAL
Cash Balance			####
LIQUIDATE INVENTORY			(see INVENTRY)
TOTAL CASH FOR 6 MONTHS			(Cash Bal. + Liq. Inv.)
LOAN PAYOFFS			####
FINAL CASH BALANCE			(Total Cash for 6 Mo. - Loan Payoff)

Job 36 continues on page 76

Task 3: Income Statement Summary

Open **INCOMEST—Final**. Follow the instructions. Save and print.

TASK 3: SIX MONTH INCOME STATEMENT SUMMARY

Open the **INCOME—Final** spreadsheet and link all six INCOME spreadsheets.
Follow the instructions below:

1. Place cursor in cell to receive July revenue link: **B7;** then key
   =July!B6--Excel
   +July:B6--Lotus 1-2-3
   Copy link formula from B7 down to B12

2. Place cursor in cell to receive Aug revenue link: **C7**; then key
   =August!B6 (Excel)
   +August:B6 (Lotus 1-2-3)
   Copy link formula from C7 down to C12

3. Continue individual column linking for the SEPTEMBER, OCTOBER, NOVEMBER, and DECEMBER revenue.

4. Enter the formula to add the TOTAL SALES for each month and copy across.

5. Place cursor in B16 and link the Cost of Goods Sold:
   =July!C15 (Excel)
   +July:C15 (Lotus 1-2-3)

6. Continue linking for the AUGUST, SEPTEMBER, OCTOBER, NOVEMBER and DECEMBER Cost of Goods Sold figures.

7. Enter the GROSS PROFIT formula (Total Sales - Cost of Goods Sold) and copy across.

8. Place cursor in B20 and link the Advertising Expense
   =July!B21 (Excel)
   +July:B21 (Lotus 1-2-3)
   Copy link formula from B21 down to B26.

9. Continue linking for the AUGUST, SEPTEMBER, OCTOBER, NOVEMBER, and DECEMBER expenses.

10. Enter a formula to add TOTAL EXPENSES and copy across.

11. Enter the NET PROFIT/LOSS formula (Gross Profit - Total Expenses) and copy across.

12. Create a line chart using Gross Profit and Net Profit/Loss.

Task 4: Line Chart Showing Gross Profit and Net Profit/Loss

Use the Gross Profit and Net Profit/Loss information from the final income statement to create a line graph showing the financial success of your business.

COMPANY NAME							
		SIX MONTH INCOME STATEMENT SUMMARY					
	July	August	September	October	November	December	
REVENUE:							
PCD140	(Link)	(Link)	(Link)	(Link)	(Link)	(Link)	
DTS500							
HCD240							
SSS200							
MDC340							
STS400							
TOTAL SALES	####	####	####	####	####	####	
Cost of Goods Sold	(Link)	(Link)	(Link)	(Link)	(Link)	(Link)	
Gross Profit	####	####	####	####	####	####	
OPERATING EXPENSES:							
Advertising Expense	(Link)	(Link)	(Link)	(Link)	(Link)	(Link)	
Payroll Expense							
Rent Expense							
Market Research Exp.							
Interest Expense							
Misc. Expense							
Total Expenses	####	####	####	####	####	####	
Net Profit/Loss	####	####	####	####	####	####	